THE
GODDESS
CASTS THE RUNES

"A revelatory reimagining of the runes that reclaims them from the grip of patriarchal myth and returns them to their roots in Goddess lore and Earth-centered wisdom. With profound insight and spiritual depth, each rune is illuminated through the lens of the Triple Goddess, offering readers not only a richer understanding of the Elder Futhark, but also a path back to the Divine Feminine."

–NICOLETTE MIELE, AUTHOR OF
RUNES FOR THE GREEN WITCH AND
THE RUNES AND ROOTS ORACLE

THE GODDESS CASTS THE RUNES

Divination & Wisdom *of the* Earth Mother

A Sacred Planet Book

ANU DUDLEY

Destiny Books
Rochester, Vermont

Destiny Books
One Park Street
Rochester, Vermont 05767
www.DestinyBooks.com

Destiny Books is a division of Inner Traditions International

Sacred Planet Books are curated by Richard Grossinger, Inner Traditions editorial board member and cofounder and former publisher of North Atlantic Books. The Sacred Planet collection, published under the umbrella of the Inner Traditions family of imprints, includes works on the themes of consciousness, cosmology, alternative medicine, dreams, climate, permaculture, alchemy, shamanic studies, oracles, astrology, crystals, hyperobjects, locutions, and subtle bodies.

Copyright © 2025 by Anu Dudley

All rights reserved. No part of this book may be reproduced or utilized in any form or by any means, electronic or mechanical, including photocopying, recording, or any information storage and retrieval system, without permission in writing from the publisher. No part of this book may be used or reproduced to train artificial intelligence technologies or systems.

Cataloging-in-Publication Data for this title is available from the Library of Congress

ISBN 978-1-64411-726-2 (print)
ISBN 978-1-64411-727-9 (ebook)

Printed and bound in the United States by Lake Book Manufacturing, LLC
The text stock is SFI certified. The Sustainable Forestry Initiative® program promotes sustainable forest management.

10 9 8 7 6 5 4 3 2 1

Text design by Virginia Scott Bowman and layout by Kira Kariakin
This book was typeset in Garamond Premier Pro with Kepler Std, Hypatia Pro, Gothiks Condensed, Haboro serif, and Gill Sans MT used as display typefaces.
Artwork by James Stewart

To send correspondence to the author of this book, mail a first-class letter to the author c/o Inner Traditions, One Park Street, Rochester, VT 05767, and we will forward the communication.

Scan the QR code and save 25% at InnerTraditions.com. Browse over 2,000 titles on spirituality, the occult, ancient mysteries, new science, holistic health, and natural medicine.

*I dedicate this book to my dear friend and mentor
Hazel "Haluna" Littlefield, who has cheered me on
during the arduous process of writing this book.
Her compassion, wisdom, and savoir faire are a beacon
of Mother Goddess energy in the world, and I want
to be like her when I grow up.*

CONTENTS

Acknowledgments   ix

PART I
Reclaiming the Runes for the Goddess

Origin of the Runes	2
Theft of the Runes	9
Casting the Runes	17

PART II
Reading the Runes
The Maiden Arc: Birthrights

1	Fehu, the Reindeer Mother: *Wealth*	30
2	Uruz, the Primal Cow: *Energy*	34
3	Thurisaz, the Giants: *Connection*	37
4	Ansuz, the Voice: *Agency*	40
5	Raidho, the Wheel: *Purpose*	43
6	Kenaz, the Eye: *Knowing*	46
7	Gebo, the Giver: *Gratitude*	49
8	Wunjo, the Wish: *Desire*	52

The Mother Arc: Challenges

9 Hagelaz, the Hail: *Disruption*   56

10 Naudhiz, the Bow Drill: *Need*   59

11 Isa, the Ice: *Immobility*   62

12 Jera, the Year: *Time*   65

13 Eihwaz, the Yew Tree: *Death*   68

14 Perthro, the Cauldron: *Mystery*   71

15 Algiz, the Swan: *Defense*   74

16 Sowilo, the Sun: *Truth*   77

The Crone Arc: Relationships

17 Teiwaz, the North Star: *Guidance*   82

18 Berkana, the She-Bear: *Support*   85

19 Ehwaz, the Horse: *Partnership*   88

20 Mannaz, the Human Family: *Unity*   91

21 Laguz, the Lake: *Wisdom*   94

22 Inguz, the Portal: *Fertility*   97

23 Dagaz, the Day: *Opportunity*   100

24 Othala, the Homeland: *Totality*   102

Conclusion   105

Bibliography   107

Index   111

ACKNOWLEDGMENTS

Many people have helped make this book a reality. I want especially to thank my artist friend Jimmy Stewart, aka Jimmy Grackle, who created images that reflect the Earth-based spirituality character of the book's contents.

Also, this book couldn't have made it to print without the kindness and patience in caring for my troglodyte self that was provided by my tech expert friend Lunar Chickadee Windbloom, who translated my writing into stuff my publisher could work with.

PART I

Reclaiming the Runes for the Goddess

ORIGIN OF THE RUNES

The runes have long been associated with the Germanic cultures of northern and western Europe. The oldest runic symbols yet discovered were inscribed on the Meldorf Brooch, an artifact unearthed on the west coast of Jutland, in what is now Denmark, dating from the middle of the first century CE. By 250 CE, runic symbols were found throughout Germanic regions, inscribed on what appear to have been talismans. By the Middle Ages, the runes had been consolidated into a kind of writing system, although one that was never in wide use. It was the rise of the Vikings during the eighth century that brought the runes to the attention of the larger world, and today many people think of the runes mainly as symbols used by the Vikings.

During the nineteenth century, Europeans experienced an occult revival and some groups in Germany saw the runes as Aryan symbols of a so-called "Master Race." The runes were later appropriated by the Nazis in the twentieth century to signify their national and racial superiority. In a few instances today, some runes are still used to symbolize white supremacy beliefs.

But the runes have another story to tell. This brief history of the runes is by no means complete, for it does not include the ancient feminist origins of the symbols that would eventually coalesce into the runic system. Understanding the runes' beginnings enables us to fully understand their rich, complex meanings and their importance to us today.

The purpose of this book is to provide an ecofeminist, Earth-based perspective on the runes that takes into account salient principles of feminism, environmentalism, and the sacredness of the Earth as well as the archaeological, mythological, spiritual, and etymological origins and significance of the runes. It reclaims the runes for the Mother Goddess, whose grace and power these ancient symbols were originally created to honor. We will learn how these symbols were developed by our ancestors over a span of tens of thousands of years, and how they reflect the totality of human experience—life's blessings, challenges, and relationships—making them a repository of the wisdom our ancestors gained from uncounted generations of living on this Earth. We will also learn how this wisdom applies to our current world as we cast the runes to answer today's life questions.

IN THE BEGINNING

Humans are believed to have originated in Africa; as the Earth's climate changed and the glaciers receded, our ancestors migrated into new regions that were previously uninhabited. Although humans developed many variations as a result of this diaspora, such as physical appearance and adaptations to new landscapes, their languages and cultures remained "genetically related," in the words of linguists and archaeologists. In time these related languages and cultures spread throughout Europe and much of Asia, and this vast inter-continental, racially diverse swath of the planet became known as the Indo-European region. Linguists now divide Indo-European languages into ten distinct, though related, branches, among them Germanic, Celtic, Italic, Greek, Slavic, and Indo-Aryan. Studies of early Indo-European cultures document a common cultural heritage as well, such as matrifocal social structures, Mother Goddess veneration, and practices of Earth-based spirituality. As we shall discover, the runes manifest this shared linguistic and cultural heritage in surprising ways.

Some scholars have characterized the runes as "embryonic writing" or, at best, as a rudimentary alphabet derived from the writing systems of the Greek and Roman civilizations. But the symbols that would become the runes existed long before these alphabets were developed. Furthermore these symbols were not created to be tools for literacy. To begin with, the word rune means "secret" or "mystery," suggesting that runes were meant to represent esoteric concepts. Evidence from archaeologists shows us that the runes resemble a number of ancient ideographs—picture symbols that represent ideas. These ideographs have been unearthed at Neolithic sites throughout the Indo-European region and appear to have been used for ritual purposes such as blessing, healing, and protection. It would be many thousands of years before these symbols would be consolidated into the wisdom system we now call the runes.

THE RUNES TODAY

Today we know the runes as a collection of twenty-four symbols that comprise the Futhark. The word Futhark is made up of the beginning sounds of the first six runes—*F, U, Th, A, R,* and *K*—in the same way that we derive the word alphabet from the first two letters of the Greek system, alpha and beta. If you were to explore the half dozen or so runic systems that had been developed by the time of the Middle Ages, you would find variations among them in terms of names and shapes. But since we are examining the runes from the perspective of Mother Goddess lore and exploring their primordial, Earth-based origins, we will only be looking at the oldest system, known as the Elder Futhark.

Unlike some of the later runic scripts, the runes of the Elder Futhark are made using only straight lines. This is because the runes were originally carved onto hard surfaces like bone, wood, or stone and it was far easier to make straight lines on these materials than to carve circles or curves. In this regard, the runes are like stick figures that symbolize ideas.

Linguists question whether there was ever any significance to the order of the runes within the Futhark. This order, however, has remained constant for well over a thousand years, suggesting that there was an original significance to its sequence. The runes have also traditionally been divided into three equal segments called *aettir* (*AY-teer*). *Aettir* is an Old Norse word meaning families or kinships, leading us to conclude that the runes in each segment are related to one another in a specific way.

The runes have commonly been depicted as residing in rows, which is the conventional way of ordering letters that are used for writing. But the runes were not originally created to be tools for literacy and were—in earlier times—found in sequences, carved into such shapes as circles and undulating loops. As I learned more about these earlier rune depictions, I began to conceive of each *aett* (singular form of *aettir*) as an arc rather than a straight line, with the three aettir arcs together making a complete rune circle.

Traditionally, each aett has been linked to a particular Norse deity—the first aett is linked to Freyja, the second to Heimdallr, and the third to Tyr. However, since the intention of this book is to reclaim the runes for the Mother Goddess, my convention is to name the three aettir arcs for the Triple Goddess—the triad of Maiden, Mother, and Crone. The characteristics of the three members of this triad help us better understand the deeper meanings of the runes that reside together within each arc.

The first arc, containing the beginning eight runes, belongs to the Maiden. The Maiden radiates the eagerness to embrace life. Her perspective is joyous, and she declares with wonder, "Look what I have! Look what I can do!" The Maiden possesses her gifts simply because she is alive, and she exudes confidence and *joie de vivre*—the joy of being alive. The runes in this arc represent the fundamental blessings we receive from Mother Earth because we are her beloved children. These blessings generally pertain to us personally, although we share them with others. The Maiden Arc can be called the Birthright Arc, and contains the gifts of wealth, energy, connection, agency, purpose, knowing, gratitude, and desire.

The second arc, comprising the middle eight runes, is the Mother Arc. Although the runes in this segment warn of challenges, these problems are given to us by the Mother to help us, not to harm us. Her perspective is stern but caring. In other words, the hardships represented by these runes are meant to guide us to become stronger, wiser, and more resilient. In a sense, they help us grow up. That is why this segment can also be called the Challenge Arc. These runes appear to be wholly negative and can make us exclaim, "Oh no! Not another learning experience!" However within each of these runes resides a valuable lesson. The problems caused by disruption, need, immobility, time, death, mystery, defense, and truth can help us mature, if we are willing to let them.

The third arc, the Crone Arc, contains the final eight runes. Like the Crone, this arc is filled with *savoir faire*—the knowledge of just what to do in any situation. The Crone holds the gifts of all the runes in her compassionate heart, and she endows this final arc with guidance, support, partnership, unity, wisdom, fertility, opportunity, and totality. She blesses us with the desire and the ability to take responsibility for our lives, build strong relationships, and foster cohesive communities. Thus this final segment can also be called the Relationship Arc. It instructs us in the many ways we can serve our friends, families, communities, and the world around us.

DEEPER MEANINGS

Up to this point, we have been examining the historical aspects of the runes. But the most important questions remain: Why did our ancestors create these symbols, and what purpose did these images fulfill?

An initial answer might be that as human consciousness developed people wanted images that could represent their evolving awareness of the world around them, especially images that signified the mysteries of life and death. The awe that was dawning on the human mind needed expression, and so people began drawing images that honored the source of their awe. These images manifested their veneration for the Mother Goddess and illustrated the understandings, experiences, and practices that would, in time, become known collectively as Earth-based spirituality.

The Mother Goddess of our ancestors was seen as the Divine Entity who created life and endowed it with strength, compassion, and wisdom. As our ancestors worked at conceptualizing this thing they called life, they observed that human life was born out of female bodies. Furthermore they recognized a parallel between human mothers and the Earth Mother, who produced all forms of life out of her body. Thus it followed that the original Divine Creator would be personified as the Mother. Our ancestors, of course, understood the necessary contributions made by males to the process of conception, but it would take tens of thousands of years before male gods would come to replace the Mother Goddess as the supreme creator of life.

To further help us identify the Mother Goddess hidden in the runes, we need to look at them from the perspective of what scholars call "feminine energy." Nel Noddings explores this concept in her book *Caring*, where she discusses what she terms the "three R's" of feminine energy—relatedness, receptiveness, and responsiveness—and looks at how these energies help structure cohesive and collaborative social systems. *Relatedness* is the understanding that everything is connected to everything else. *Receptiveness* is what helps us be open to and experience that connection. *Responsiveness* enables us to act on these connections. In addition, Noddings suggests that the fundamental impulse of feminine energy is to "tend and befriend," an impulse that nurtures a community and holds it together. This impulse is in contrast to what she calls the "fight or flight" tendency of male energy, which, although important in certain situations, does not in itself nurture a community and bind it together.

Regardless of our gender, all of us possess feminine energy, not just those who identify as female. Feminine energy is "process" energy, the kind of energy each of us uses every day to keep things flowing. At its most basic, process energy is experienced in things like breathing, eating, and walking, or feeling, hearing, and knowing. In contrast, masculine energy is "goal" energy. When we need to accomplish a task, we enlist goal energy and summon it up out of the flow of process energy. When the task is achieved, goal energy subsides back into the flow of process energy. Alas, over the millennia society has come to idealize masculine or goal energy and devalue feminine or process energy. As we explore the runes, we will discover the many and diverse ways in which they manifest feminine energy.

Feminine energy is also found in the practices of Earth-based spirituality, where the Divine is experienced as present in the here and now, rather than in some "heavenly," far off, nonphysical realm. The Earth and all her creatures contain Divine energy, for Spirit dwells within each of us. Thus the path of Earth-based spirituality leads us to experience the Divine in present time and space by our relatedness to all beings and through our receptiveness and responsiveness to these relationships. As we shall discover, these Earth-based spirituality precepts find expression in the meanings of the runes, for they are the principles and ethics of the Mother Goddess.

So far, we have been exploring the origin of the runes and their relationships to the Mother Goddess. But for well over a thousand years, Odin-centric mythology has dominated interpretations of the runes. Odin rose to be the chief god of the Norse pantheon, and most people think of the runes in the context of Odin as their possessor. In the next chapter, we will look into Odin's story and revisit the narrative of Odin's appropriation of the runes.

THEFT OF THE RUNES

One morning at breakfast, as I was working on a crossword puzzle I came across a clue that made me curious about the runes. The clue was "Odin's prize." I was familiar enough with Germanic mythology to know that Odin's prize was the runes. This information is written in the *Hávamál*, a group of poems found in the *Edda*, a collection of Scandinavian myths and legends compiled by Icelandic scholar Snorri Sturleson in the thirteenth century. As I pondered the clue, four questions took shape: First, who was this Odin who had won the runes? Second, how had Odin managed to win the runes? Third, who had the runes originally belonged to? And finally, why did Odin want to win the runes?

WHO WAS ODIN?

Odin is a familiar character in Norse mythology. He is commonly portrayed as a muscular white male with a thick mane of hair and a full beard, wearing an ornate breastplate and a horned helmet and carrying a spear. In this guise, he is God of Battle, Lord of Hosts, Giver of Victory, and God of the Dead. But Odin is also pictured as a black-cloaked traveler with a wide-brimmed hat pulled down over his face, slipping silently among the shadows. In this persona, he is God of Magic, God of Poetry, and God of Runes, who sacrificed one of his eyes to gain occult wisdom.

10 ～ *Reclaiming the Runes for the Goddess*

Despite his prominence in mythology, however, Odin was a relative newcomer to the Norse pantheon. It was not until the fourth century CE that a figure called Odin first appeared, and it was only during the Viking Age, when the Norsemen began driving their waves of conquest over Europe starting in the ninth century, that Odin attracted wider attention. The earliest tales of Odin showed him to be an unsavory character. He was dishonest, untrustworthy and malicious, a swindler and an oath-breaker, and a source of evil who promoted strife among tribes and kinsmen and reveled in discord.

The tale of how Odin stole the Mead of Inspiration is a good example of his treachery. It was the giant, Suttungr, who possessed this magical brew, and Odin set out to steal it so he could acquire its occult wisdom for himself. On his way to Suttungr's stronghold, Odin encountered nine thralls, or laborers, who were reaping hay for Suttungr's brother, Braugi, and he tricked the thralls into killing one another. Odin then sought lodging for a night with Braugi, who complained that he had no workmen to harvest his hay fields. Odin gave his name as Bolverkr—Evil Doer—and offered to do the work of the thralls in exchange for a sip of Suttungr's legendary mead. Braugi agreed to this bargain without consulting his brother. Thus when the work was done and Odin demanded his drink of mead, Suttungr refused.

Suttungr kept the Mead of Inspiration in three great cauldrons hidden within a secret cave. Odin drilled into the cave to steal the mead, but when he entered it he found Suttungr's daughter, Gunnlod, guarding the cauldrons. He set about seducing her, and after three nights he asked for a sip from each of the three vessels. Gunnlod agreed, but instead of sips, Odin took three enormous gulps and drained all three cauldrons dry. Then he changed himself into an eagle and flew away to Asgard, the home of the Aesir gods. As recounted in the *Hávamál* (stanzas 104–110), Odin boasted, "Gunnlod gave me a drink of the precious mead . . . I let her have ill payment for her loyal heart and faithful love . . . the fraud-got mead has profited me well."

Why would the Vikings elevate such a treacherous character to be their chief god? Perhaps they saw Odin's malicious behavior as a model that validated their own marauding enterprises; he glorified warrior culture and legitimized self-serving activities. Later, under the influence of the new religion, Christianity, Odin's image was cleaned up a bit to make him appear to be a benefactor of mankind and he was subsequently referred to as All-Father. As literacy spread during the Middle Ages, people elevated Odin still further as God of Poetry, the One Who Bestowed Inspiration. After all, hadn't he "acquired" the Mead of Inspiration and made it his own?

HOW DID ODIN WIN THE RUNES?

The *Hávamál* (stanzas 138–39) used Odin's own voice to tell this story:

> *I know I hung*
> *On the windswept tree*
> *For nine full nights in all,*
> *Wounded with a spear,*
> *And given to Odin,*
> *Myself to myself,*
> *On that tree*
> *Of which none know*
> *From what roots it rises . . .*
> *I peered down,*
> *I grasped the runes,*
> *Screeching I grasped them,*
> *And fell down from there.*

This story is reminiscent of the crucifixion of Christ, who sacrificed himself upon a tree-like cross to save humanity. The story also alludes to the ancient shamanic practice of climbing up an arduous tree-like

Mjotvidr, the Mother Tree, from which the runes ripened and dropped to Earth

path to the spirit world to seek help for those in need. However, while Christ and shamans sacrificed themselves to gain salvation and healing for humanity, Odin merely engaged in a self-serving ritual whose only purpose, in my view, was to get the power of the runes for himself.

If we just focus on Odin's so-called sacrifice, though, we miss the significance of the nine nights during which he hung on the tree. Nine is a number sacred to the Mother Goddess: nine equals three times the Triple Goddess of Maiden, Mother, and Crone. Nine is also a number sacred to women in pregnancy, as it takes nine months to grow a new life. Odin hung himself for nine nights to symbolize a period of gestation, and after nine nights, Odin "birthed" his new god-like self. And the fact that Odin hung himself for nine nights rather than nine days is also meaningful. Hesiod, the third century Greek poet, called night the "Mother of the Gods," suggesting that it was the night that held the mysterious power of creation rather than the day. By counting his ordeal in units of night, Odin symbolically usurped the role of the Mother Goddess as creator.

TO WHOM DID THE RUNES
ORIGINALLY BELONG?

After nine nights, Odin looked down, saw the runes upon the ground, and grabbed them up in his hand. This tale suggests a parable of a hero's quest, a hero who was alone in the wilderness, seeking enlightenment. But Odin was not alone. There was also a mystical being—the windswept tree upon which he hung—and it was to this tree that the runes belonged.

In traditional Norse mythology, the windswept tree is called Yggdrasil. But long before Odin renamed the tree Yggdrasil and claimed it for himself, it was known as Mjotvidr (*m-YOT-vee-theer*), the Mother Tree. Veneration of a Mother Tree is ancient and universal, and can be traced at least as far back as Neolithic times, when she was also known as the World Tree, the Tree of Life, and the Tree of Knowledge. Mjotvidr was the fabled Axis Mundi, whose roots reached deep into the Underworld, whose trunk passed through the core of the living world and whose branches stretched into the heavens and were hung with stars.

Mjotvidr becomes an important prop in Odin's hero tale, securing his dominance. At the same time, the Odin myth diminishes the tree's significance by declaring that Mjotvidr was just a tree whose roots were unknown. But Norse mythology had long before established that Mjotvidr arose from three roots which reached out over the entire earth. Humans, the myth tells us, lived under one root, the gods lived under another, and the Goddess Hel, the keeper of the Underworld, lived under the third. Furthermore, Mjotvidr's roots were deeply embedded in the Earth, from which all life, all time, and all wisdom arose, making the Mother Tree a majestic emanation of the Mother Goddess herself.

And what of the runes that lay upon the ground beneath Mjotvidr? They were emblems of Mother Earth's power and wisdom which, like ripened fruit, had dropped to the earth from her branches. The runes symbolized the Earth Mother's gifts to all living beings, and were spread upon the ground so that all who had need of her sustenance, protection, and guidance could have access to them.

WHAT DOES ODIN'S THEFT OF THE RUNES SIGNIFY?

If the riches of life, symbolized by the runes, were freely given to all beings, why did Odin have to hang himself on Mjotvidr to get them? Some might argue that, in typical hero fashion, Odin sacrificed himself in order to gain the knowledge of the runes. But I think there is another answer that lies in the runes' spiritual, Earth-based, and feminist origins, and which represents a turning point in the human experience.

A few years ago, I taught a course at the University of Maine entitled "History of the Goddess," where we covered the tens of thousands of years in which humans had venerated a Mother Goddess. As historians and archaeologists have discovered, our ancestors appear to have lived in peaceful and prosperous gynocracies—matrifocal communities governed by women—which had modeled themselves on the relationship between mothers and their children. Gynocratic societies distributed their resources to equally benefit all members of the community, not just an elite and powerful few.

But around six thousand years ago, these harmonious human communities started to experience profound disruption. We are learning that climate change may have been one of the factors, causing things like desertification in some regions and flooding in others, forcing humans to adapt their societies to severe changes in land and environment. We know little about these displaced Indo-European peoples, but it appears that some groups found it expedient to adopt warlike characteristics in order to survive, and they began conquering peaceful matrifocal societies, gradually destroying gynocratic cultures over a period of several thousand years. Male rulers and pantheons of male gods appeared, and with them came war and systems of hierarchy, misogyny, slavery, and a new ethic of "might makes right." The Mother Goddess was cast down, mirroring a simultaneous decline in the status of women in society as the new male gods and rulers seized the Mother Goddess's authority for themselves.

These ancient conflicts happened long before societies became literate and were able to write down their histories. Instead, our ancestors incorporated many of these events into their oral traditions, and many of these stories were eventually retold as myths in which goddesses and gods acted out human events on a grand mythological stage. Confrontations between the old matrifocal cultures and the new patriarchal regimes were translated into dramatic sagas of heroic gods vanquishing dark and dangerous goddesses.

16 ～ *Reclaiming the Runes for the Goddess*

And so it was with the story of Odin and the runes. Odin's appropriation of the runes, his theft of these ancient symbols, acted out patriarchy's overthrow of the Mother Goddess and her societies of cooperation, generosity, peace, and equality, replacing these with warrior culture and the ascendancy of male gods.

Having explored the historical, mythological, and spiritual foundations of the runes, let us now examine the ways we can reclaim these ancient symbols for the Mother Goddess and explore how they can help guide us as we move through the unknown territories of our lives.

CASTING THE RUNES

The word casting can have different meanings or connotations; we think of casting a spell or casting a fishing line. Casting runes is somewhere in between! We use the phrase "casting the runes" because we literally drop the runes onto whatever surface we are using. We then use their meanings and our intuition to apply them to the question at hand.

There are so many different types of sets of runes available that you have many options. I have a number of rune sets. In one, the runes are flat round pieces of ceramic with the rune images etched into them. Another has the rune images engraved on flat squares of bone. I made a set from slices of a deer antler I found in the woods, and one of my students crafted me a set of wooden staves—the runes' original form, made of small, flat sticks of beech wood. There are even sets of rune cards.

CASTING THE RUNES AS CEREMONY

One way to look at casting the runes is that you are performing a ceremony, one in which you ask for information from the Invisible Realm— the World of Spirit—using techniques of divination. Divination is the practice of foretelling future events or discovering hidden knowledge by using occult or supernatural methods. Since the runes' images were originally created to symbolize esoteric concepts, they are well suited to the task of divination.

At the start of a rune casting ceremony, I like to ground and center myself and call in Spirit to guide me and to influence which runes come forth. I invite the person I am reading for to do the same. In this way, we align our energy with our intention, which is to receive an answer to the question. Then we ask that the right runes come into our hands to give us the information we are seeking. Next, we interpret the answers that the runes have given us. Finally, we end the ceremony and thank Spirit and the runes for their assistance. Of course, this ceremony can be shaped in other ways too, depending on your own practice, the question being asked, and the person asking the question.

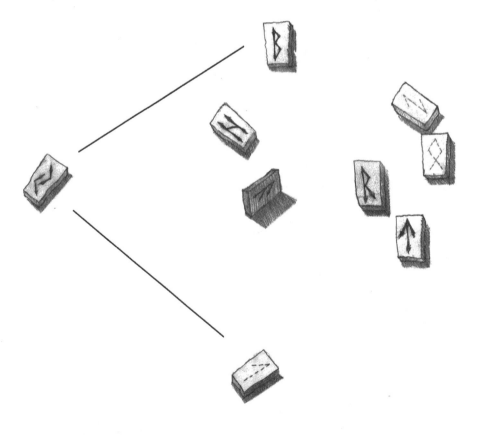

An example of a rune casting

CREATING THE QUESTION

Casting the runes is done for the purpose of answering a question, and before any reading of runes can take place, you need to carefully craft your query. What do you want to know? Creating the question is often the most difficult step in the casting and needs to be done with deliberation because a well-crafted question will draw forth the best runes for the reading. The question also provides the lens through which the runes will be interpreted.

Some people may ask a question that requires a simple yes or no answer, but the runes that appear may expand on that, giving you more detail. When people ask specific questions, they generally receive clear answers. A vague question, on the other hand, might only receive a vague answer. I have been asked to do readings on questions that were not well thought out, with the result that the answers were often unsatisfying. It has often been said that, on some level, we already know the answer to the question we are asking. The runes simply help us bring this answer into our conscious awareness.

SELECTING THE TOOLS

We have begun by stressing the importance of the question. But, of course, unless you have a set of runes, you won't be able to do a rune casting. You will need to find a set of runes that you can relate to. As described above, a set of runes might take many different forms. How do they look to you, their size, color, and shape? How do they feel in your hands? How do they sound as they clink together when thrown down? You may want to try a few different sets before deciding on the one you feel most resonant with, or you may want different sets for different situations.

It is customary to cast the runes onto a rune cloth, like an altar cloth. This rune cloth is generally laid out on the ground, putting the runes in contact with the Earth—the source of wisdom. The cloth is ideally a two-foot round or square piece of smooth, heavy white or light-colored fabric, which helps frame the casting and make it more visible. Be sure that whatever surface you are casting upon is as smooth and level as possible. Be alert to the fact that casting onto a hard surface like a floor or table can sometimes make the runes bounce a little when they land, which could affect their positions in the reading.

CASTING THE RUNES

To begin, you need to select the runes for the casting. State the question, and invite the most helpful runes to come forward to answer it. Some rune casters reach into their rune bags and, without looking, pull out a certain number of runes. Others allow the person asking the question to do the selecting themselves. Generally, I like to let people pick their own runes. I tell them to close their eyes, concentrate on their question, and grab a handful of runes. I often suggest taking nine runes because nine is a sacred Goddess number, but the person asking the question can make their own decision about how many to choose. After they select the runes, they put them into my waiting hands. When doing the casting, I generally like to face north, the direction of the Elders and Earth wisdom. Standing as I hold the selected runes, I repeat the question out loud and declare, "May this reading be true." Then I bend down and, with my hands about a foot above the ground, drop the runes all at once onto the rune cloth.

After the runes have landed, I look at the overall shape they have made on the rune cloth. Sometimes they form the outline of a particular rune, thus suggesting an initial focus and helping to establish a theme for the reading. Or the runes may create the shape of some image, one that can also inform the reading. If no shape is apparent, that's fine too, and you can just proceed.

Next, I examine the position that each rune has landed in. How many of the runes are face up and unobstructed so that their images are entirely visible? These are called "bright" runes. Bright runes are generally fairly simple to interpret; they are what they say they are, and their meanings are usually straightforward.

When a rune has landed face down so that the image is hidden, it is called a "dark" rune. Dark runes are more complicated. First of all, it needs to be understood that every rune which appears in a reading has an effect—whether it is dark or bright. If it had nothing to offer, it would not have bothered to show up. It is important to remember that all runes, including dark runes, are best understood when examined in the context of the question and the positions of the other runes.

At its most basic, a dark rune might be saying that the rune's quality is not available at this time, though it may come to bear with regard to the question or situation sometime in the future. If a positive rune, like Fehu (Wealth) or Uruz (Energy), lands in the dark position, this could mean that, while the benevolent quality of the rune is available, you are unable to recognize it or accept it at this time. Or, in the case of a rune from the Challenge Arc, for example Hagalaz, Rune of Disruption, a dark position might be saying that its meaning

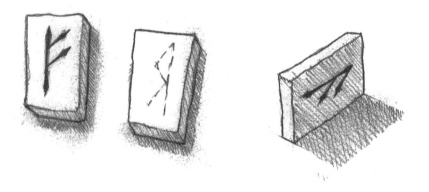

Recognizing "bright" and "dark" runes in a casting

is even darker than originally thought—an intensification. On the other hand, it could be saying that the meaning of this particular rune is not really as bad as it seems. A dark rune could also be expressing the opposite meaning. For example, a dark Eihwaz, the Death Rune, could mean resurrection rather than death. Or it could be telling you that the urgency is blunted and the prognosis is not as bad as it seems. If a positive rune, like Thurisaz/Connection or Ansuz/Agency lands in the dark position, this could mean that, while the benevolent quality of the rune is available, you are unable to recognize it or accept it at this time. How will you know which interpretation is accurate? In the end, again, dark runes are best understood when examined in the context of the question and the positions of the other runes.

Another possibility is that a rune has landed balanced on its edge. In this case, the meaning of that rune could go either way—it might be "bright" or "dark," depending on other factors influencing the question. This is another example where the question and the positions of the other runes help clarify the meaning.

Often, however, one rune lands on top of another one. Overlapping runes add even more complexity to a reading. This configuration generally indicates that the rune on top must be dealt with first before the

An example of runes clumped together

rune underneath can manifest. This can be even more challenging if the overlapping rune is dark.

Other possibilities are that the runes may have landed clumped together. Runes in close proximity to one another may suggest a conglomerated meaning, so that they could be better understood as a group rather than by their individual meanings. And alternatively, if a rune lands off to the edge of the casting, it could be suggesting something in the future, or something that has only a remote likelihood of manifesting at all. Here, more than ever, the nature of the question, plus the runes' relationships to each other, will help determine the answer.

Finally, notice which arcs the runes belong to. As discussed earlier, I am dividing the runes into three arcs: the Maiden Arc, the Mother Arc, and the Crone Arc. Runes from the Maiden Arc signify positive birthright blessings. Those from the Mother Arc warn of challenges. And runes from the Crone Arc refer to our relationships. Is there a preponderance of runes from one particular arc, or a scarcity, or are the arcs evenly represented? These observations can provide additional insight.

The image on the next page is an illustration of a rune casting I did for myself to find out how my upcoming eye surgery would turn out. I was relieved that the runes predicted a generally good outcome. Fittingly, the shape of the overall casting looked like Kenaz, the Eye Rune, which was gazing toward a cluster of other runes, suggesting that these clumped runes would have something to tell me about the surgery and its outcome. I will walk through my interpretation of this rune casting briefly as an example, but note that detailed descriptions of each rune and their meanings appear in the next part of this book, "Part II: Reading the Runes."

Beginning at the top of the "eye," Berkana, Rune of Support, told me that I would receive the support I needed from my community to get through the surgery and recovery period. Hagelaz, Rune of Disruption, predicted that the procedure would understandably cause quite a disruption in my life, while Jera, Rune of Time, advised that,

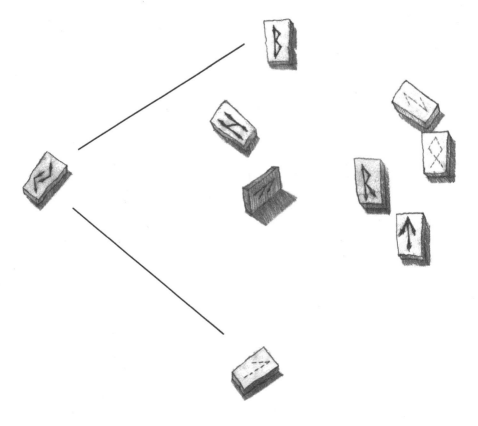

The rune casting in response to the author's question

as long as all was done at the proper time and in the proper manner, the procedure would be successful. The rune at the center of the focus of the "eye," Ansuz, the Voice Rune, had landed on its edge, telling me that I would need to speak up about what I needed regarding the procedure and recovery period, and that my willingness or reluctance to speak up would have an influence on the outcome. The rune at the lower point of the "eye" was Laguz, Rune of Wisdom, but it was in a dark position. I worked for quite a while at understanding this rune, and finally concluded that, given my reluctance toward change, it would be some time before I fully appreciated the wisdom of my choice to undergo the surgery.

The "eye" was looking at a cluster of four other runes. Eihwaz, the Death Rune, was also dark, but in view of the general positiveness of the casting, I took this to mean that, rather than an abrupt end to my ability to see, I would experience just the opposite—the return of good, clear vision. Othala, the Rune of Totality, another dark rune, suggested that the world would eventually open up to me in new ways, but I had to be ready to see it. Raidho, Rune of Purpose, assured me that I was on the right path of good self-care, and Teiwaz, Rune of Guidance, confirmed that I had made the right decision to undergo the procedure. Incidentally, the surgery was successful, and I gained practical, emotional, and spiritual wisdom about the meaning of sight in my life.

UNDERSTANDING THE RUNES

We cast the runes to get answers to our questions, and we tend to want clear, straightforward answers to help us navigate our complicated world. Students have said to me, "Just tell me the right answer! Don't make me think!" However when we are dealing with the complexities of our lives, it is rare to find simple answers to our questions. Rather, we must think about the information at hand, reflect on its significance to the situation, and construct the best answer we can in the moment.

The discussions in Part II of this book provide historical, spiritual, and mythological explorations of each rune. These explanations are meant to help you get to know the runes, and to establish relationships with them so you can understand their "language," especially when it gets interpreted in the context of the questions being asked and the contributions being made by the other runes in the casting. Hopefully, you will come to appreciate the various nuances of meaning that the runes offer in different situations. With the runes, as in life, we need to come to our own conclusions in order to find our most meaningful answers. And while we may rely on the guidance, support, and resources of our communities to find these answers, we must still take responsibility and be actively involved in the process ourselves.

The understandings we receive when casting the runes come from a good, solid intellectual grasp of the runes' meanings gained through learning and practice. But in the end, this learning must always be filtered through our own experiences, empathy, and inner knowing—our gut feelings. Sometimes we have to rely on our instincts rather than our intellect, even if we can't explain our insights rationally. Ultimately, our intention must always be to act for the greater good and with an understanding of the free will of all so that our readings are helpful, as well as compassionate and wise.

May all your readings be true.

PART II
Reading the Runes

As explained earlier, the runes are divided into three arcs or *aettir* (families). With our goal of reclaiming the runes for the Goddess, we are naming the three arcs for the Divine triad of Maiden, Mother, and Crone, also called the Triple Goddess. The runes of each arc share characteristics with the member of the trio who embodies the arc.

The Maiden Arc
Birthrights

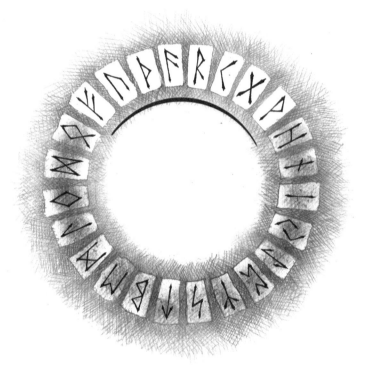

The first arc is that of the Maiden; it is also called the Birthright Arc. The runes of this arc are emblematic of the gifts Mother Earth has bestowed upon us simply because we are children of the Earth, including wealth, energy, connection, agency, purpose, knowing, gratitude, and desire.

I. FEHU, THE REINDEER MOTHER: *WEALTH*

The wealth of life is symbolized by the rune Fehu (*FAY-oo*). The word Fehu is related to the Old Norse word *fjol* (*fYOL*), translated as "many" or "much." This makes Fehu the Rune of Wealth, the wealth that is ours simply because we are alive, for life is the greatest wealth of all. On a mundane level, however, the dictionary defines wealth as a great quantity of material things, like money, property, or other possessions, and this is how we typically think of the meaning of the rune Fehu.

For thousands of years, wealth was equated with cattle, those domesticated herds of bovines that provided our ancestors with meat and milk. The domestication of cattle fundamentally changed human societies and gave them a way to measure material wealth. However, in the ancient cultures of the North this wealth was embodied not by cattle, but by reindeer. Indeed, the shape of Fehu is an ideograph for the pronged antlers of reindeer, not, as some suggest, the curved horns of cattle. Thirty-five thousand years ago, there were such vast herds of reindeer roaming the plains of the North that historians named this period the Reindeer Era. But the people of the Reindeer Era did not own the reindeer. Rather, they followed the seasonal migrations of wild reindeer herds across the land. People sustained themselves on the wealth given by the reindeer, and the reindeer sustained themselves on the wealth provided by Mother Earth.

An animal of this much importance to human survival inevitably entered the realm of the gods, and so the reindeer came to be revered

Fehu, the Reindeer Mother, Creator of Life and Wealth

as a divine being, an avatar of the Mother Goddess. Like the rest of the vast deer family, reindeer became symbols of birth and the creation of life. Our ancestors venerated numerous reindeer goddesses, such as the Evenki goddess Bugady Musan and the Scandinavian goddess Disa, both of whom were honored as Mothers of the Universe. The goddess Beiwe was the Saami people's Reindeer Mother, who traveled through the sky each day in a sleigh made of reindeer antlers. The Saami also revered Sar-akka, another life-giving reindeer goddess.

It is important to note that the female reindeer have antlers as well as the males. Thus ancient cave paintings of reindeer (without male genitalia) and reindeer skulls enshrined at ceremonial sites, shown genetically to be female, tell us that our ancestors venerated the reindeer doe. And field research shows that it is the oldest female who guides the reindeer herd over the land to food and safety. Thus the reindeer that pull Santa's sleigh are likely an ancient folk memory of these pathfinder does, who wended their way unerringly across the night sky with their sleigh overflowing with wealth.

Fehu reminds us that we are wealthy just because we are alive. Therefore, Fehu can also be called the Rune of Life. As writer John Ruskin wrote, "There is no wealth but life." Fehu asks us to recognize all the kinds of wealth we have that support our lives, because wealth abounds.

How does Fehu help answer the question?

Looking at Fehu's wealth from its broadest perspective, this rune's appearance in a casting is telling you to celebrate the blessings of being alive, for what greater wealth is there than life itself? Fehu's presence also encourages you to live your life consciously and enthusiastically, to recognize and embrace the wealth of life that is all around you.

On a more prosaic level, Fehu is usually seen as indicating some form of material wealth that is coming your way. With Fehu, projects can be financed, homes can be bought, education can be funded, and all the other things that need money or material resources can now happen.

The exact nature of this wealth, of course, will be understood in the context of the question you are asking, and so you must first determine how wealth relates to the question. For example, are you trying to deal with a specific need for wealth and how to get it, or how to best use the wealth you have now?

What if Fehu is "dark" or covered by other runes? This could mean that the wealth you seek is not available at this time. Alternatively, Fehu may be telling you that the wealth you need is present, but you just don't recognize it. Perhaps you should examine your life more closely so you can see the wealth that is all around you.

2. URUZ, THE PRIMAL COW: *ENERGY*

Uruz (*OOR-ooz*) represents the energy we need in order to live our lives. The energy of Uruz enables our hearts to pump blood through our bodies, and our lungs to inhale and exhale the air we need to breathe. Uruz energy fuels all the things we do with our bodies. Without Uruz energy, we cannot live. Therefore Uruz can also be called the Rune of Health, for our bodies need Uruz energy to function properly.

In the mythologies of many cultures, Uruz energy issued from the Primal Cow in the form of her sacred milk that fed the gods and all other beings. Indeed, the Primal Cow and her energy were considered so essential to life that she was installed in the pantheons of many cultures. In India, she was called Aditi, the Mother of the Gods, who sustained them with her divine milk. Cow-Eyed Hera, the Greek Mother Goddess, fed the Titans and the Olympians. The ancient Egyptians honored the goddesses Hathor and Isis, who were depicted as having cows' heads and offering their milk-filled breasts to the world. In Norse mythology, the Primal Cow was Audumla, who fed Ymir, the progenitor of the giants, with her four rivers of milk.

The name Uruz comes from the Old High German word *ur*, meaning "existing from the beginning." The term is also the root of the Germanic word *urohso*, which was the name of the ancient bovines now known as the aurochs. Aurochs were enormous wild black cattle, six feet tall at the shoulder and weighing upwards of a ton. Aurochs fossils have been found dating back a million years, and the vast range of aurochs, from Scandinavia to the Indian subcontinent, coupled with their legendary ferocious energy imprinted them in myth as well as human memory.

The best-known prehistoric representation of aurochs is a cave painting at Lascaux made some thirty thousand years ago. It shows a huge aurochs leaping over a herd of horses, illustrating its indomitable energy. Depictions of aurochs also emphasized their long horns that curved forward, as though projecting their energy out into the world. We frequently associate horns with bulls, but aurochs cows also had horns, as did the cows of many cattle species. And while today we tend to think of the bull as representing energy, the vital energy of life originally emanated from the Primal Cow and her divine milk.

Some believe that the shape of Uruz represents the lowered head of a bull projecting his energy toward the earth. But it would be more historically and mythologically accurate to see Uruz's shape as an ideograph for Audumla, the Primal Cow, walking across the land. The vertical line depicts one foreleg planted on the ground, while the diagonal and shorter lines represent her other foreleg lifted in the process of taking another step forward, powered by her vital energy. Uruz tells us that whatever we need to do in our lives, the energy of the Primal Cow is there to help us.

How does Uruz help answer the question?

The energy represented by Uruz is what we need to live our lives, and since Uruz is situated in the Maiden Arc, its Birthright energy is wholly positive. Uruz is suggesting that you have the vital energy you need for whatever you are attempting to do.

The specific kind of energy represented by Uruz will be clarified by the question being asked, along with the other runes. Therefore, what does energy have to do with the question? What kind of energy is needed? A "dark" Uruz might be asking if you actually have the energy to engage in a certain task. Is this the right time to go ahead

36 ～ *Reading the Runes*

with a project, or would it be wiser to put it off until the energy needed is stronger or better suited to the task? If this is the right time, however, then Uruz is encouraging you to go ahead, wholeheartedly, and get the job done.

Uruz is also the Rune of Health. How does your physical health relate to the question?

3. THURISAZ, THE GIANTS: *CONNECTION*

The name Thurisaz (*THOOR-i-saz*) comes from the Old Norse word *thurs*, meaning giant. The giants were the original inhabitants of the Earth, the children of Jord (*YORDH*), the Earth Mother. They lived for ages because Jord's blood flowed in their veins. Giants were enormous beings, yet they were gentle and peaceful, beautiful and wise. They embodied the forces of nature, shaped the mountains, valleys, rivers, and coastlines, and placed the ancient stone megaliths upon the landscape. In Norse mythology, the giants were known as the Vanir gods, venerated as vegetation and fertility deities. The giants were also the ancestors of humans, making them our primordial great-grandparents.

But this halcyon era of the giants and their peaceful, harmonious world came to an end when, as Norse myth tells us, the Vanir were attacked by invaders from the east called the Aesir. This has been confirmed by historians to have occurred around 2000 BCE. During this conflict, which was known in myth as the Vanir Wars, the giants staunchly held their own against the Aesir, who, in the end, were forced to concede with a truce. But through acts of trickery and treachery, the Aesir eventually managed to break the truce and impose their warrior culture upon the Vanir. In Norse myth, the invaders became known as the Aesir gods, and the defeated giants were gradually demeaned as immoral and destructive beings.

By the Middle Ages, fairy tales disparaged the giants even further by depicting them as ugly and stupid. In the end, Thurisaz became equated with a thorn, instead of a giant. After all, the pointed shape of Thurisaz looked like a thorn, and a thorn seemed a more appropriate symbol of protection in a Christian world than an ungodly giant. Nevertheless, the shape of Thurisaz was originally meant to be an ideograph of a giant. Since runes were drawn using only straight lines, the angular protrusion from the middle of the rune's vertical line was meant to represent the curve of an enormous body—the torso of a giant.

Thurisaz is the rune that helps us inhabit the world outside of ourselves. We may feel unsure, confused, or even unsafe when dealing with the complex world around us. But when we reach out to the giants, they take us by the hand, like the primordial great-grandparents they are, and walk with us, teaching us the ways of the world and keeping us safe. Thurisaz assures us that we are not alone.

In this regard, Thurisaz can also be called the Rune of Protection. We may hesitate or stumble, but the giants are ever with us. They pick us up, comfort us, and help us move on. They also shield us from the consequences of our inexperience, lack of knowledge, and poor judgement. They embody the solicitous spirit of Mother Earth, and help us interact with nature and all the other beings that live in the world. Indeed, feeling connected to the world outside of ourselves is our greatest protection, for our well-being and survival depend upon it.

How does Thurisaz help answer the question?

As one of the positive Birthright runes, Thurisaz is telling you that you are safe and can go forward with confidence. You are not alone, and you can rely on your "inner giants" to protect you, advise you, and help you to feel connected to the world around you.

But you must look to the question to truly understand the deeper meaning that Thurisaz is presenting. For example, is the question touching on a risky or uncomfortable situation which is calling for some kind of reassurance? If it lands "dark," could it be saying you are unsure of yourself and in need of encouragement or forgiveness, or that you are being troubled by some unresolved issue that is keeping you from getting on with your life? If so, the giants are here to help.

An even deeper question is this: What do the "giants" mean to you? Do they embody the spirits of nature and of the land? Have you worked at deepening your connection to these entities so you can experience their care and protection as you face the outside world? In the end, Thurisaz is about awareness of what is going on around you—physically, energetically, emotionally, and spiritually—and the giants are your allies in helping you become aware of these connections.

4. ANSUZ, THE VOICE: *AGENCY*

Ansuz (*AHN-sooz*) is our voice, one of our most important gifts because it establishes our presence in the world. With our voices, we articulate our thoughts, feelings, desires, and intentions. To have a voice means we are expressing our opinions to others. To be a voice suggests we are speaking up for some idea that is important to us. Our voice is a manifestation of our individual identity, our persona, our creative Self. It represents our agency in the world and signifies our ability to shape our lives and influence those around us.

Ansuz is often called the Mouthpiece of the Gods. The shape of the rune, a vertical line supporting two shorter downward slanting lines, depicts the open mouth of a divine being speaking the Sacred Word to the world. However, the name Ansuz contains the Indo-European root word *an*, which originally meant Mother Goddess. Indeed, there are so many goddesses whose names begin with or contain the syllable *an*, as well as place names honoring goddesses, that they could easily fill an entire page in this book. This makes *an* originally a designation for the Goddess. Therefore Ansuz is more accurately called the Mouthpiece of the Goddess.

What issues forth from the Goddess's Mouthpiece is her sacred voice. Early on the voice was conceived of as the agent of creation, for the Goddess's Voice brought forth everything in the universe simply by speaking its name. In fact, the word "voice" comes from the name of the Vedic goddess Vac, the Creator Goddess who spoke the world into existence. Eventually the voice of the Goddess found expression in other cultures and was personified in such goddesses as Sarasvati, Chokmah, and Sophia. The idea of voice as a divine creative agent also found its way into the Bible, where it was written, "In the beginning was the word."

Our ancestors sought the voice of the Goddess in order to advise them on matters of importance, and women were most often her mouthpiece. The connection between women and the voice of the Goddess seems to have been established early on among Germanic peoples, and it was the custom to regard women as endowed with the gift of prophecy. In Norse tradition, it was the *spamadr*, or prophecy woman, who conveyed the Goddess's voice to the community. And anthropologists and historians tell us that the shamans of our ancestors were originally women and they channeled the voice of the Goddess to answer the questions of their communities.

Ansuz is also known as the Rune of Communication. While we may at times seek the voice of the Goddess for information and wisdom, we need to remember that Ansuz also represents our own voice and embodies our own ability to communicate. Ansuz reminds us that our voices give us agency and that we can use them to create and influence the world around us. People know us by our voice, and Ansuz suggests we use that voice with care, for it has great power and consequence. But communicating is a two-way street, and Ansuz is also about our ability to listen to what others are saying to us.

How does Ansuz help to answer the question?

Because it is one of the positive Birthright runes, when Ansuz shows up in a casting it is sending the message that you have something important to say that will help address the question. Ansuz may also be suggesting that your voice represents your ability to handle the issue at hand, and that you have a significant part to play in the resolution of the problem by speaking up and saying what is on your mind.

42   ~   *Reading the Runes*

On the other hand, Ansuz could be warning that you are not able to speak meaningfully at this time. If Ansuz is dark, perhaps you should keep quiet, because speaking up might complicate the situation. It could also be telling you to listen to what is being said to you, for there may be information spoken to you that could help answer your question.

We must also be open to the possibility that the voice referenced by Ansuz is not your own voice, but that of Spirit. If that is the case, then Ansuz may be telling you to listen to this voice so it can help answer your question. You might hear the voice of Spirit through your intuition or inner knowing, or it may come to you through divination or your skills of clairaudience or telepathy.

5. RAIDHO, THE WHEEL: *PURPOSE*

The name Raidho (*RAY-tho*) comes from the German word *Rad*, meaning wheel. The wheel is one of humankind's most important inventions, and has contributed to society's technical progress since ancient times. Besides assisting in transportation, wheels have served as the basis for many rotary mechanisms such as water wheels, windmills, and grindstones. And beyond its practical applications, the wheel became a symbol of rolling along our path, fulfilling our life's purpose.

Implicit in the wheel is the characteristic of continuous movement, for the wheel, like life itself, is not a static disc, but turns around a central point. The wheel reminded people of the daily path of the sun, the monthly journey of the moon, the yearly turning of the seasons, and the annual migration of the constellations around the heavens. Because of this rotational quality, the wheel became a symbol of the cycle of life. Many moon goddesses, including the Welsh goddess Arianrhod, whose name means Silver Wheel, embodied this cyclical path around the universe's center.

The name Raidho is also related to the Old Norse word, *radh*, meaning council or advice, and the Anglo-Saxon word *rede*, meaning road or way. Raidho poses two existential questions that all of us must answer at one time or other in our lives. The first is, "Where do I want to go?" The second is, "How shall I get there?" These questions are ultimately answered by having a sense of our life's purpose. And our purpose is driven by our will. Will is the faculty of conscious, deliberate action and the power to choose those actions that fulfill our purpose. The old Wiccan Rede states, "An' it harm none, do what ye will." This means that, without harming anyone, we must use our will to choose and follow our path in life. But what council guides us on our path?

The Norse believed that individuals determined their paths using *mattr ok megin*, the inner counsel they received from the Mother Goddess. This counsel was the center around which the wheel of their lives revolved. Another factor that influenced them was *orlog*, the Norse version of karma. Orlog is not fate, where the gods decree the course of our lives and we must obey. Instead, orlog represents the accumulated consequences of decisions we have made and experiences we have chosen, even those decisions and experiences from past lives. Be they fortunate or unfortunate, it is the consequences of our orlog that direct our wheels and shape our present and future paths.

Although some see Raidho's shape as the letter R, it is actually an ideograph of a person walking along a path, head facing forward, with one leg lifted to take the next step on the journey of life. Raidho, the Wheel, represents us following our path, acting out our will and fulfilling our purpose. Hopefully, we are listening to our *mattr ok megin* so we can travel the path we have chosen for ourselves.

How does Raidho help answer the question?

Raidho is a positive rune, and it is most likely indicating that you are on the right path. In this case, Raidho is signaling a "green light" on your life's journey. The direction you have chosen is a good one and will lead to a positive outcome.

On the other hand, Raidho may be asking if you are on the path you want to be on, or whether you know what path you are actually on? If Raidho is dark, are you lost? Are you on this path by default because you don't know where else to go, or has it been forced upon you? Perhaps Raidho is telling you to look around and get your bearings before going any further on this particular path. You may need to clarify your purpose in life.

Another explanation for Raidho's appearance is that you are going to take a journey somewhere. But life itself is a journey, and so it is important to have a broader view about your life's itinerary. Raidho could be asking you to check in with your *mattr ok megin*, your inner guidance, to be sure that your sense of purpose is congruent with the path you are on.

6. KENAZ, THE EYE: *KNOWING*

The name Kenaz (*KEN-az*) comes from the German word *kennen*, to know. Kenaz represents our intelligence, the rational capacity of our minds to think and acquire knowledge and understanding. The shape of Kenaz, a chevron, is an ideograph for an open eye looking out at the world. Together the eye and our intelligence signify conscious awareness, and form a partnership that enables us to perceive what is going on around us and derive meaning from it.

While the eye provides us with our physical sense of sight, it also symbolically gives us the ability to understand our world. It is an icon for perceiving the meaning of things beyond their material reality. There is a saying, "seeing is believing," meaning that seeing something with our own eyes gives it reality. But our intellect also has "eyes" that give us the ability to understand ideas. We say, "I see what you mean," or "I see this in a new light," when we comprehend the deeper meaning of something. We also use the metaphor of seeing when we understand something well enough to take charge of it, like when we "see to it," or commit to "keeping our eye on it." In this sense, seeing implies that we are making sense of the situation and doing something useful with that understanding.

The chevron shape of Kenaz has very old Goddess roots, and from ancient times it was a symbol of the Eye Goddess. On statuary and pottery, the Eye Goddess was depicted with chevrons bracketing her wide-open eyes and cascading down to Earth, representing her all-seeing vision and wisdom. And the eye itself was a goddess symbol in many cultures. The Egyptian goddess Maat, the Mother of Truth, was represented by an elaborate eye image, and the eye was also an Egyptian hieroglyph that meant "to know." The eye represented the Celtic Sun Goddess, Sulis. Her name came from the Gaelic word *suil*, meaning eye and sun, and one of her titles, Suileath, meant all-seeing, far-sighted, and wise.

There is an interesting connection between the concepts of knowing and sexuality that is embedded in the word Kenaz, for *kennen* and Kenaz are both derived from the Indo-European root word *kunda*, meaning vulva, the female genital opening. The Old Norse version was *kunta*, and in English it became *cunt*, slang for vagina. The word *cunt* is related to the word *cunning*, meaning shrewdness or having secret knowledge. Secret knowledge was originally thought to reside in the Yoni of the Universe, the Goddess's sacred vulva. It was believed that women naturally possessed this knowledge because of their gender, and men could access it through sexual intercourse with women. Temple priestesses, called harlots, provided men with this access through the sacrament of sexual union with the Goddess. And in the Tantric practice of kundalini, men sought enlightenment through spiritual sexual connection with the Goddess. Therefore, as the Rune of Knowing, not only does Kenaz represent an open, all-seeing eye, but also the Goddess's open legs, inviting access to her sacred knowledge.

How does Kenaz help answer the question?

When Kenaz shows up in a casting, it may be saying that you see what is going on and you can handle the situation. Since Kenaz is a Birthright rune and is basically positive, it may bring a sense of relief about your ability to figure out the answer to the question.

Kenaz might also raise various questions. What do you actually know about the problem? What do you need to know in order to address it? How will you go about getting this information? Are you able to understand or make sense of the situation? A dark Kenaz could be saying that you can't see anything in regard to the question.

Kenaz might also be the most important rune in the reading because it might signify a "Holy Grail"—a sudden epiphany that helps you finally understand an essential point regarding the question. It might give you an "aha" moment in which you will gain an important insight. On a purely mundane level, Kenaz may be suggesting a sexual connection that will have an impact on your life.

7. GEBO, THE GIVER: *GRATITUDE*

The name Gebo (*GAY-bo*) comes from the German word *geben*, meaning to give. The act of giving presupposes a gift, and a true gift is given without expecting anything in return. The non-reciprocated nature of a gift makes it different from an exchange, where one expects to receive something of equal value. But if we are not going to get anything back, why do we give?

We can begin to answer this question by looking at some of the goddesses who share Gebo's name, such as the Alagabiae, "Those Who Give Richly," the group of Germanic goddesses whose role was to give of the abundance of the Earth. There were also the Norse goddesses Gefn, "The Giver," who gave the gifts of the sea, and Gebjon, "The Giving One," who tended Freyja's sacred treasure chest of abundance. These goddesses embodied the Earth as the eternal and unconditional giver. Why does the Earth give? She gives because she is a loving mother whose deepest desire is to nurture her children and see them thrive. The Earth's instinctive urge to give is done without expecting anything in return, but simply out of love, the most important impetus for giving a gift.

The "X" shape of Gebo is an ancient symbol associated with the Mother Goddess. It was derived from the simple equal-armed cross icon that signified the Earth's strength and stability. When tipped sideways, this Earth cross became an X, the so-called "cross saltire" or "tumbling cross," and was thus transformed into an activated Earth symbol that

50   ~   *Reading the Runes*

depicted its energy flowing in the world. The X, or cross-band as it has been labeled by archaeologists, was found inscribed on early pottery and goddess figurines, signifying the gift of life-sustaining energy. In this way, the shape of Gebo represents the ancient tumbling cross that continuously gives to the world. We still use the X symbol today to suggest the giving of a loving kiss, or to mark the spot of buried treasure.

As children of the Earth, we are natural givers, and we contribute to the "tumbling cross" of Earth energy simply because we are alive and part of the flow of life. And we continuously give to the world around us, even if we are not conscious of doing so. For example, our exhaled breath gives carbon dioxide to the plant world, and when we die our bodies decompose and give their nutrients to the soil.

We can intentionally give to the world around us with our gratitude, sending out our gratitude for things like sunrises and rainbows, beautiful music and interesting books, sweet babies and close friends, for having enough food to sustain us, safe homes to shelter us, and communities that care about our well-being. Gratitude is the greatest gift we will ever have to give. It arises naturally from our hearts and asks for nothing in return. When we give the gift of gratitude, we honor all the gifts we have ever been given. Like the "tumbling cross" of Gebo, our gratitude flows on in the world and gifts others with its love.

How does Gebo help answer the question?

Another Birthright rune, Gebo is positive and implies a good outcome. Perhaps you are being given a gift, or you might be the one giving the gift to someone else. Either way, Gebo's appearance is saying that giving has some bearing on the question being asked.

Alternatively, Gebo could be asking if you are able to give at this time. Are you feeling fearful of letting go of resources, or that others are not deserving of your gifts? Fundamental to Gebo is the idea of gratitude. Gratitude is a gift that we give to the world, without expecting anything in return. We also feel gratitude when we are fully present and aware of the world around us. Gebo may be reminding us that we need to give more attention to feeling gratitude in all aspects of our lives.

Gebo is often called the Marriage Rune because, when we wed, we say we are giving ourselves to each other. We may extend this idea of giving of ourselves to any relationship that is deeply important to us.

8. WUNJO, THE WISH: *DESIRE*

The name Wunjo (*VOON-yo*) comes from the German word *Wunsch*, meaning a wish. Wunjo gives us the blessing of desiring things that enrich our lives, and that is why Wunjo is often called the Wish Rune. It signifies the ability to want the things that life has to offer. Desire is a natural and healthy impetus that propels us forward in our lives. It motivates us to seek new relationships, develop new skills, and go after new experiences that can make our lives fuller and more satisfying.

Wishing is actually just a simple form of magic, and Wunjo can also be called the Rune of Magic. Many people engage in magic without realizing it. This is because both wishing and magic are simply the combining of a desire with some sort of ceremony, no matter how small, and then sending it out into the universe to be fulfilled. An example of a time-honored method is to state the wish out loud while focusing on an object that is believed to bring good luck. This object might be a shooting star in the night sky, a candle flame flickering on a birthday cake, or a fountain of gushing water. The ceremony could be as simple as closing one's eyes, or blowing out the candles, or tossing a coin into the fountain while concentrating on the wish. The star, the flame, and the fountain are simply touchstones that help us align our energy with our desire so we can make our wish come true.

The name Wunjo honors the Wunschen Weiber, or "Wish Women," an ancient Matronae group of Germanic goddesses who granted wishes. There were wishing goddesses in other cultures as well, such as the Norse group called the Oskmeyjar, or "Wish Fulfillers." The power of these wish-granting goddesses has lived on in fairy tales as the fabled Fairy Godmother. She was the wise and compassionate one who waved her wand and granted the wishes of those who were deserving and sincere.

Fittingly, the shape of Wunjo is an ideograph of the Fairy Godmother's magic wand. The rune's wand-like vertical line is topped with a triangular emanation that signifies the flow of energy streaming from its tip toward the wish. The wand has always been considered a tool for the fulfillment of wishes, and was used by priestesses to channel the power of the Mother Goddess. Wunjo is also called the Fairy Flag because of wishing's association with Fairies. And its shape can also be seen as a fairy's magical banner waving in the breeze.

Regardless of whether or not we believe in magic, it's good to acknowledge the importance of wishing and desire. After all, desire is one of our birthrights. Desire is given to us by the Mother Goddess to help us want the things that make life worth living. The hardest part of wishing may be knowing exactly what to wish for.

How does Wunjo help answer the question?

In the best of outcomes, Wunjo is saying that your wish is about to come true. In this context, wanting something is a positive thing because wishing is life-affirming. To desire something means that you are alive and want to continue to enjoy the good things life has to offer, as the Mother Goddess intends. Wunjo might also be suggesting that it's time to perform some magic.

Wunjo might also be asking you to clarify your desire. What do you really want? Knowing what you desire makes it more likely that you will be able to figure out how to get it. Does your desire have a specific form, or is it more of a feeling? Are you simply wishing for something instead of actually going out and doing what is necessary to make it happen?

Finally, are you open to having your wish come true even if it does not materialize in the exact form you had envisioned? Sometimes the best manifestation of a wish can be a complete surprise, one that you couldn't have imagined, but one that nevertheless fulfills the essence of the wish. When wishing, it's often best just to be clear on how you want to feel, and let the universe handle the details.

The Mother Arc
Challenges

The Mother Arc, the middle eight runes, speaks to the challenges we encounter as a path to growth. Disruption, need, immobility, time, death, mystery, defense, and truth comprise this Challenge Arc; they may show up as negative elements, but they have much to teach us as we rise up to address them.

9. HAGELAZ, THE HAIL: *DISRUPTION*

The name Hagelaz (*HAY-ge-laz*) comes from the German word *Hagel* (*HAY-gel*), meaning hail. Hail is a weather phenomenon described as a showery precipitation of ice pellets that range in size from less than an inch in diameter to over four inches. Driven down from the clouds by strong winds, hailstorms can be very destructive because when they are powerful enough they can destroy crops, damage buildings, and kill livestock. In addition, hailstorms are sometimes accompanied by thunder and lightning, making them seem even more threatening. The disruption brought about by hail can cause fear and despair, in addition to material damage that may demand considerable time and effort to repair.

Many rune casters say that the shape of Hagelaz represents the letter H for Hagel, or hail. But the runes were created long before the Germanic peoples became acquainted with the Roman alphabet, so the meaning of Hagelaz's shape has to come from an earlier source. First of all, unlike the letter H, the two vertical lines of the rune are linked by a diagonal line rather than a horizontal one. Second, this horizontal line suggests a slanting bridge leading from a higher point to a lower one. The most famous bridge in Norse mythology was the mythical Bifrost, the Rainbow Bridge that connected Asgard, the realm of the gods, to Midgard, the domain of humans. Bifrost was guarded by the god Heimdallr, who prevented humans from ascending to Asgard. But the gods themselves were free to move back and forth on this swaying road

The Mother Arc: Challenges ～ 57

to heaven whenever they wished, bringing their other-worldly energies down to the Earth plane. Sometimes these energies were benevolent, but often, as many Norse myths recount, they were disruptive, much like a formidable hailstorm.

But hail brings with it an interesting contradiction because, after the hailstorm has passed, its ice pellets melt into the earth, nourishing the soil. An old Anglo-Saxon rune poem speaks to hail's dual nature:

> *Hail is the whitest of grains.*
> *It is whirled from heaven's loft,*
> *Tossed about by wind gusts,*
> *Then melts into water.*

Thus hail, seemingly an attack from the heavens, could bring unexpected benefits. In the rune poem, hail is referred to as "the whitest of grains," in other words, as seeds. Therefore Hagelaz could bring the seeds of change, sowing new possibilities on the disrupted soil of one's life.

The primary message delivered by Hagelaz is that a disruptive event is about to happen, a disruption that alters the normal course of one's life. This disruption inevitably leads to change, and we rarely welcome unexpected and disruptive change. But without change, we stagnate. Disruption, and the change it brings, can lead to new growth when, like hail, it drops into our lives and seeds our future.

How does Hagelaz help answer the question?

When the hailstorm of Hagelaz hits, expect some sort of disruption to your accustomed ways of doing things. This disruption could merely feel disconcerting, upsetting your usual routine and making you temporarily adjust how you are doing things until you can figure out how to get back to normal. Or it might seriously disrupt your current plans, making you take a detour so you can get where you want to go by an

58 ～ *Reading the Runes*

alternate route. In any event, you are left picking up the pieces, clearing away whatever debris is left behind, and figuring out how to resume life as before.

In the Challenge Arc, however, a "dark" Hagelaz might be saying that the disruption is even worse than it appears on the surface. But it could also be suggesting the reverse, that there is really no disruption at all, and we are simply imagining it. What do the other runes have to say?

Remember, Hagelaz's disruptive challenge could also bring an unanticipated benefit, if you can be open to it and not just throw up your hands in dismay. By the time the storm passes, you may have discovered a better way of doing things, or perhaps gain an understanding of how to prevent this disruption in the future. Hagelaz's chaotic interruption may be sowing the seeds of a better way to go about your life in the future.

10. NAUDHIZ, THE BOW DRILL: *NEED*

The name Naudhiz (*NOW-theez*) comes from the Old Norse word *nauth* (*NOWTH*), meaning need. It is also cognate with the German word *Not*, translated as the misery and distress caused by dire need. Need is different from want. We all have wants. These are desires for things we believe will bring us happiness or make our lives more comfortable. But need is more serious. It arises when a sudden and drastic loss challenges our survival, such as a loss of food, shelter, or safety. While unsatisfied wants may lead to disappointment, needs left unmet have more serious consequences and must be attended to immediately because they are critical to our existence.

Need creates worry and fear. But need can also drive us to search for solutions to the very problems that are causing that worry and fear. An old rune poem reminds us:

> *Need constricts the heart,*
> *But it often serves as a help and salvation*
> *If attended to in time.*

This is why Naudhiz is called the Need-Fire Rune. A need-fire is a rapid fix to an urgent problem, and is sought in troubling situations where solutions must be created quickly. It is produced by combining fast thinking with whatever materials and resources are readily available.

The meaning of the shape of Naudhiz is in dispute among rune casters. It is simply an ideograph for a bow drill, an ancient tool for starting a fire. This was an important invention for our ancestors because it enabled them to make fire whenever they were challenged with a need for heat, light, or protection. A bow drill is operated by vigorously rubbing two sticks together to produce a spark that ignites a fire. The shape of the rune's vertical line crossed by the diagonal line represents these two sticks.

A certain amount of luck may also be involved in creating a need-fire, which is why, when faced with a tricky situation, we sometimes make the need-fire sign with our fingers by crossing the middle finger over the index finger, and saying "wish me luck." This gesture looks similar to the shape of the bow drill rune, and is meant to add a spark of luck to the task at hand.

Need creates the incentive to fix a problem, which leads to a useful solution. As the old saying goes, "necessity is the mother of invention," for need frequently gives birth to a remedy. This is why Naudhiz resides in the Mother Arc. Just as Nat, the nurturing Germanic Goddess of Night, gave birth to Dag, the glorious Goddess of Day, so the deprivations and perils of need can bring forth shining solutions. When Naudhiz appears in a rune casting, it signals the presence of an urgent need. But Naudhiz also prompts us to invent a quick solution that can help us meet the challenge that has suddenly confronted us. If we can create the need-fire, then we are on the way to resolving the problem.

How does Naudhiz help answer the question?

When Naudhiz shows up, it is alerting you to a serious need that has arisen which must be attended to immediately, otherwise you may face serious consequences. The rune is telling you that you can't put off dealing with it. And a dark Naudhiz might be warning that this need is even worse than you thought.

The Mother Arc: Challenges ⌇ 61

How are you going to handle it? Are the other runes warning that an answer to the question is unattainable because a solution cannot be found at this time? Or are they saying that other factors must be dealt with first before the need can be met? Defining the nature of the need will be one of the things to figure out because, once the need is clearly articulated, Naudhiz suggests you may be able to invent a way to deal with it quickly. Remember that while Naudhiz signifies serious need, it also represents the possibility of creating a solution that remedies the need—some kind of an ingenious need-fire. This need-fire may be subtle or it may be straightforward, but it is most likely within your means to create it. The other runes in the reading will help you figure out how to do this.

Finally, Naudhiz is sometimes called the Rune of Luck, so its appearance in the casting may be indicating that you are going to be lucky in regards to the outcome.

11. ISA, THE ICE: *IMMOBILITY*

The name Isa (*EE-sah*) comes from the Old Norse word *is* (*EES*), which means ice. When winter envelopes the land, water freezes into ice, changing from a free-flowing liquid to an immobile solid. When used as a life metaphor, the challenges that make us freeze like ice also prevent us from acting, thinking, or feeling, even in situations where our well-being depends upon some kind of response. After all, to be alive implies movement, and the immobility of ice mimics a death-like state.

The shape of Isa is generally seen as the letter *I* for ice, and is often interpreted as an icicle. But Isa was also the name of the ancient Indus River Valley goddess who was known as the Ten Directions of Space. Rather than immobility, Isa represented the inexorable movement of time through eternity and the perpetual flow of energy in all dimensions. She propelled the cycles of life, death, and rebirth. And when we understand the dynamic way in which ice itself is formed, we can begin to appreciate the deeper implications of being frozen.

Although the end result of freezing appears to be paralysis, the process that produces and maintains ice is an active one, involving constant movement. As the ambient temperature of the air drops, the water at the surface cools and becomes denser and heavier. As a result, this heavier water sinks, causing the warmer water beneath to rise to the surface. Then this new surface water cools and sinks as well, in an increasingly accelerated cycle. If the ambient temperature remains cold enough, the surface water freezes into sheet ice, insulating the water underneath and enabling it to circulate even faster. This process adds more and more ice to the underside surface, increasing its thickness. There is a lot of creative movement happening beneath the surface of a frozen lake that is not apparent to an observer watching from shore.

The Vedic goddess Isa eventually found her way to the Northern European pantheon as the Disir (*DEES-eer*), a group of guardian goddesses who oversaw the well-being of society. One of the avatars of the Disir was the serpent, a universal icon of the Mother Goddess. Every mythology has a World Serpent who encircles and protects the Earth. The Norse had the Midgard Serpent, who wrapped herself around the Earth to guard it. Knowing the Disir's relationship to the World Serpent, we can see Isa's single vertical line as an ideograph for the Mother Serpent who, when the living world is challenged, clasps it in her powerful embrace to protect it.

Although ice can be a metaphor for immobility, its stillness can also symbolize the process of inner growth and healing that is going on beneath the frozen surface. While chilling adversity may stop us in our tracks, it may also offer us a pause which, like the encircling embrace of the Mother Serpent, can give us time to reassess our situation and refocus our energy so we can arise refreshed when winter, or the situation causing us to freeze, has finally passed.

How does Isa help answer the question?

When Isa shows up in a casting, it is indicating that some aspect of your life is frozen. You are unable to take action, make decisions, or respond appropriately to what is happening. You are in the grip of something stronger than yourself and, twist and turn as you will, you can't seem to break free. Whatever question you have asked, Isa is telling you that you are being prevented from acting upon it, and for the time being you simply must resign yourself to the situation.

Perhaps the question itself may suggest what kind of immobility you are facing, or the other runes may help you understand how or

64 ～ *Reading the Runes*

why you are frozen. However, there is nothing you can do about it at present. You've just got to wait until the ice breaks up.

But maybe you are frozen because you need a rest, a pause in the way you have been doing things. This frozen state may be giving you a chance to meditate on the way your life has been going, and on how you want it to be in the future. Stillness has its uses. The process of freezing into ice is an energy-intensive one—it took a lot of energy to get you stuck; that very energy, and the patience and acceptance the state of being frozen demands, could be working in a revitalizing and restorative way, if you will allow it to do so.

12. JERA, THE YEAR: *TIME*

The name Jera (*YAIR-ah*) comes from the German word *Jahr* (*YAR*), meaning year, a cycle of time. A cycle is a series of recurring phenomena that happen in a particular order so that whatever the cycle is representing can function as it is meant to and achieve its purpose. When the cycle reaches its end point, it simply begins again. Some cycles happen naturally, like the circle of seasons. There is also the respiratory cycle, where the actions of breathing in and breathing out happen spontaneously, even when we are asleep. But some cycles require conscious effort, like those created by humans. One such cycle is the agricultural year, in which the challenges of planting, watering, and weeding crops must be diligently attended to at the correct time and in the proper manner to ensure a successful harvest. The challenge of Jera is to pay attention to the passage of time and use it wisely in order to achieve your goals.

The word Jera has ancient goddess roots which connect the rune to the concept of cycles and time. The Near Eastern goddess Jerah embodied the monthly cycles of the moon and the yearly cycles of the sun. She was descended from the Vedic goddess Jara, who ruled the cycles of time and transformation, perpetually producing the elements needed to sustain life. The shape of the rune Jera is an ideograph for cycles, and thus for the passage of time. While most rune shapes are made with vertical lines that anchor them to the ground, Jera's shape suggests continuous movement above the ground as its chevrons move around a central point of time.

66 ～ *Reading the Runes*

Jera is sometimes called the Rune of Harvest, referring to the bounty that is achieved after a successful agricultural cycle. But the bounty implied by such a harvest is not Jera's principle meaning. Instead, the focus of Jera is time, with its cycle of responsibilities that must be done in proper sequence so that whatever harvest is being labored over can be accomplished. Thus Jera might more accurately be called the Rune of Time Management.

The task of accomplishing a harvest is not just about getting crops in, however. It can also be a metaphor for spending the time and doing the tasks needed to achieve any type of goal. Doing the right work, in the right order, and at the right time can be very challenging for those doing the work. Challenges may come from external problems that interfere with the process and may be beyond our control. But challenges can also come from self-induced problems like taking shortcuts or procrastinating—in other words, from not honoring the importance of time. Jera signifies the need for planning, commitment, and follow-through. If we are willing to take the time required to fulfill our plans, then the harvests in our lives can be good ones. How we spend our time will largely determine the quality and quantity of whatever "harvest" we are working toward.

How does Jera help answer the question?

Our lives are measured in segments of time, and the concept of time often carries with it various responsibilities. We are admonished to not waste time and to spend it wisely, as though it were a currency that we use to get what we want in life. We may feel like we never have enough time, or that time creates a rat race, with no commensurate satisfaction.

How does time impact the question you are asking? Is how you are spending your time satisfying to you? Do you feel like your timing is off in some aspect of your life? Is time marching on, insensitive to those joyous or poignant moments that you wish could last forever? Or is time weighing heavily on your hands, challenging you to get through those hard moments that seem to go on without end?

On the other hand, Jera's message might be that time is on your side, provided that you fulfill your responsibilities "in good time." If you are paying attention to the cycle of time and its requirements, then you may very well receive a successful harvest from your endeavors. It depends on what the other runes are saying, and how sensitive you are to the value of time in your life.

13. EIHWAZ, THE YEW TREE: *DEATH*

As the Death Rune, Eihwaz (*EYE-waz*) may seem like the most formidable challenge we have to face in the Mother Arc. The idea of death can trigger terror, sorrow, and regret, for it signifies the loss of something in our lives, gone forever. Death comes to everyone, and all things must end eventually, and we are now faced with trying to figure out how our lives will go on in the face of this irrevocable loss.

But all is not necessarily lost when Eihwaz appears—it may simply be transformed into some other state of being, for the name of the rune comes from the Old High German word *Iwa* (*EYE-wah*), the yew tree. The yew tree symbolizes eternity and perpetuity beyond death. Our ancestors believed that the spirit that enlivened their bodies did not vanish at death but instead transitioned into new beings. In many cultures yews were planted in cemeteries to bestow their essence of regenerated life on those who had passed on. This was partly because of the yew's remarkable longevity; there are yew trees estimated to be thousands of years old alive today. And it was also due to the yew tree's unique way of regenerating itself, according to Fred Hageneder in *The Meaning of Trees*, by recreating its core. While death comes to all beings, the yew tree reminded people that death was not an end of spirit, but simply a transformation of the body that enabled life to continue beyond the grave in some new way.

Historians suggest that Mjotvidr, the Mother Tree of Norse mythology, was modeled on the yew tree and its energy of perpetuity.

Many tribes honored the yew's regenerative powers by calling themselves the People of the Yew. Some examples were the Eubores of Western Europe and the Iberians of Spain. Ireland also venerated the yew tree, for its name comes from the Celtic word *Ierne*, meaning Yew Island. Furthermore, in addition to being honored in the runic alphabet, the yew tree was also included in the ogham, the "tree alphabet" of the Druids, where it was called Eoh (*YO*). The Irish goddess of the Underworld, Eo-Anu, embodied the qualities of the yew because she ruled over death, regeneration, and eternal life.

Eihwaz signals an abrupt end of something in one's life, the death of something that can never be regained. But the death symbolized by Eihwaz does not necessarily mean the end of a mortal life. It can indicate a point where something in our lives is changed irrevocably from one state of awareness, identity, or purpose to another.

The shape of Eihwaz, too, shows that the flow of life energy does not end at death, but is merely redirected. The long vertical line represents Mjotvidr, the Eternal Yew Tree, our own Tree of Life. The short angled lines that emerge from the top and bottom of the tree trunk represent the end of an old direction in our lives and the start of a new direction that will lead us onto some yet unknown path and transform our lives permanently. After all, without death to clear away the old and outworn, how can anything new find a place in our lives?

How does Eihwaz help answer the question?

Eihwaz, the Death Rune, is telling you that something is coming to an end. It is over, finished, and will not return. This death might be literal and refer to a mortal demise. However, it is more likely to signal the termination of something that has been very important to you, such as a job, a living situation, or a relationship—anything that could impact you in a challenging way and bring an end to a critical aspect of your life.

But remember, Eihwaz, the Yew Tree, is not only about death, but also about regeneration and redirection. When something dies, something new comes in to take its place. The consequences that arise from this death could take you in a totally new direction. But you must allow this new thing to unfold. The loss implied by Eihwaz might feel like a tragic or insurmountable challenge to you, but when you are able to recover from your grief and be open and curious about new possibilities, there will be a new life that awaits you.

14. PERTHRO, THE CAULDRON: *MYSTERY*

Perthro (*PAIRTH-ro*) is called the Rune of Mystery, for we cannot fully know what its appearance represents. Perthro signifies the Great Unknown, and we humans don't do very well in this mysterious realm. How to handle the unknown in our lives can be a tremendous challenge because the uncertainty and fear it evokes can make us feel out of control, unsure of how to act, or how to make sense of the situation.

The shape of Perthro is often equated with a dice cup tipped on its side, from which the dice have just been cast. This image suggests that life is a gamble, and therefore unpredictable. But since there are only a finite number of possibilities that can occur when rolling out the dice, there is no real mystery, just a predictable number of outcomes. A more apt description of Perthro's shape is the Great Cauldron of Norse myth, tipped on its side and spilling its contents out onto the earth. Perthro actually represents Hvergelmir, the Roaring Cauldron, in which were brewed the mysterious substances of life. What is bubbling in the cauldron is a mystery, and even when it pours out into our lives we cannot fully understand it.

Perthro is named for Perchta, the Germanic Mother Goddess of the North. She was one of the "many-sided" goddesses who inhabit multiple dimensions simultaneously. She was honored at the Winter Solstice in her role as ruler of the Underworld of Death and Regeneration. Wearing her dark cloak of wild nature and turbulent storms, Perchta led the Wild Hunt of ghostly riders who galloped through the night sky and howled with the winter wind. But she was also honored at the Summer Solstice in the guise of her alter ego, Berchta, who was venerated for her benevolence and fecundity. In this sunny aspect, she invented flax and the creative arts of spinning and weaving, and endowed the summer with warmth, rain, and gentle breezes. The mystery was how Perchta, trailing the fierce storms in her wake as she galloped through the nights of winter, could also bless the lands with abundant crops and fertile herds in summer.

There were other "many-sided" goddesses in whose cauldrons bubbled mysterious brews, such as the Welsh goddess Cerridwen, with her simmering cauldron of wisdom. The mysterious Russian goddess Baba Yaga traveled over the land each day riding in her magical cauldron. And the dark Dutch goddess Mother Holle hid her cauldron at the bottom of a deep well to catch those who fell into it. It was a fearsome experience to encounter these mysterious goddesses and their cauldrons because one never knew what would happen as a result. Would they be cooked and devoured or forced to toil endlessly in dark caves, or would they be blessed with riches and good fortune? The ways of the cauldron are unknowable. In the cauldron bubbles the potential for all things, and we cannot begin to understand what it is brewing until it pours out into our lives. And even then. . . .

How does Perthro help answer the question?

Among the most difficult of challenges is having to navigate the unknown. The unknown may be as simple as not knowing the answer to a question. But that is hardly a mystery, for all you have to do is locate the answer. Much harder is not knowing what the question is. Another mystery could be that there is some unknown factor standing in the way of a clear resolution, but you have no idea what that factor might be, and no means of finding out. In a rune reading, Perthro says it is impossible to know all of the aspects impacting the question, and therefore one is not able to fully anticipate or understand the final outcome.

The Mother Arc: Challenges ～ 73

When Perthro shows up in a casting, it is warning us that some unknowable factor is affecting the question and none of the other runes can help clarify the situation. But don't despair, because this mystery factor could turn out to be partly or even wholly beneficial rather than detrimental. You just don't know because Perthro is a mystery. All you can do is try to understand the situation as best as you can, be prepared for as many potential outcomes as you can think of, and wait to see what finally comes pouring out of the cauldron. And even then. . . .

15. ALGIZ, THE SWAN: *DEFENSE*

Algiz (*AHL-geez*) is the Rune of Defense. It warns that an adversary is threatening to attack, and that our well-being, safety, and security are suddenly in danger. This threat forces us to identify our attacker and find a way to fend off the assault.

When our ancestors found themselves under attack, they called upon the Mother Goddess, who defended them as a mother protects her children. In later eras the Mother Goddess would often be portrayed as a war goddess, dressed in helmet and armor and carrying a spear or sword. But she was originally envisioned as the Bird Mother, protecting her nestlings with beak and claw, and detecting danger with her large, staring eyes that could see into all dimensions.

When an attack was imminent, the Bird Mother often took the form of a swan. This was a natural choice because of the swan's great strength and its ability to travel in many different realms. For one thing, the swan is the world's largest waterfowl. This enormous bird can measure over five feet in length, with a ten-foot wingspan. Furthermore, the swan's wings are so strong that they can break the bones of anyone unwise enough to provoke a defensive attack. It is equally at home on water, on land, and in the air; the swan swims confidently and majestically and flies long distances at great altitudes with slow, powerful wing beats, And when walking on land, it warns of its presence with a loud, cacophonous voice, leaving some of the largest footprints of any bird. The Swan represented a powerful defender against attack.

The origin of the name *Algiz* is debated among rune casters. The word is not derived from *Schwan*, the German word for swan, but is instead related to the German words *Allgegenwart*, meaning omnipresence, and *allgewaltig*, which means omnipotent or all-powerful. Omnipresence and omnipotence are essential attributes of a defender. In ancient murals, many goddesses were portrayed riding upon swans to symbolize their great power. And the Swan Maidens, the fearsome goddesses of Germanic myth, would don their swanfeather cloaks and fly to Earth to defend those who had called out for their help.

Some would argue that the shape of Algiz represents the defensive antlers of an elk, or alternatively the sharp blades of elk sedge, a marsh grass—hence another name sometimes used for this rune is Elhaz, suggesting an elk. But the runes already have an antler symbol in the reindeer image of Fehu, and marsh grass as a defender doesn't pose much of a threat. However, images of the Bird Mother as defender have been found in archaeological sites dating back tens of thousands of years. These figures depict the Bird Mother standing erect, her head looking out over the world to detect danger, while her powerful wings reach up to the sky in a gesture of defense. This stance perfectly describes the shape of Algiz, where the vertical line signifies her head and body, and the two upward-pointing lines depict her outstretched wings defending against attack.

How does Algiz help answer the question?

When the outstretched wings of Algiz appear in a reading, be prepared for an attack of some kind and for the need to defend yourself. This could be a literal attack that you must guard against in order to protect yourself from harm, or it could be an attack on some aspect of your life. Who is attacking you, and why? What does attack have to do with the question you are asking? Identifying the nature of the attack is crucial before any defense can be mounted.

A "dark" Algiz could compound the threat, implying that it is too strong at this time and that no defense is available. It could also mean that the threat is a false one. The other runes in the reading will assist you in locating the attacker, and they may help you counter the attack.

Despite the challenge you are facing, however, Algiz may be telling you that you have a defender that can come to your aid. Who might this protector be? And what might such a defense look like, especially in the context of the question? With presence of mind and strength of heart, you will be able to summon Algiz to your side to defend you against the attack.

16. SOWILO, THE SUN: *TRUTH*

Sowilo (*soo-WEE-lo*), the Sun Rune, represents the Triumphant Self. As the final rune in the Mother Arc, Sowilo celebrates the problems we have dealt with and the experience we have acquired. Sowilo is often considered to be a positive rune. It bestows a sense of well-being and pride and promises success in our endeavors. With Sowilo, we step into the bright sunshine and declare "I Am," for we have accomplished good things and can celebrate ourselves unreservedly.

However, behind the confidence that emanates from Sowilo's golden rays lurks the question, "*Who* am I?" While self-assurance is inherent in the Sun Rune, this self-assurance must be grounded in self-awareness, otherwise the sunshine symbolized by Sowilo may only be a dazzling disguise to hide self-doubt.

The agony of self-doubt is one of the fundamental challenges of Sowilo. The other challenge is self-deception or self-delusion. As the Rune of Truth, Sowilo demands that we live by the age-old dictum of "Know Thyself." We must be honest with ourselves and others. Are we stepping into the brilliant light of well-earned acclaim, or are we just fooling ourselves? Do we secretly worry that we have been cast into the harsh light of self-examination or, worse, public scrutiny, and forced to confront the truth about who we really are? What secrets are we hiding? Do we truly know ourselves and love the person we know ourselves to be? Equally important is the question of whether we are telling the truth.

78 ～ *Reading the Runes*

Although the sun has been gendered male for several thousand years, originally the solar orb was venerated as the Sun Mother, and the name Sowilo is related to those of a number of sun goddesses throughout the Indo-European world. For example, there is Sol, the Scandinavian "Mistress Sun," and Saule, the Baltic Sun Mother, and of course Sunna, the Teutonic sun goddess from whom we get our word *sun*. But the name Sowilo is most closely linked to the Celtic sun goddess, Sulis (*SOO-lis*), derived from the Celtic word suil (*SOO-eel*), meaning sun.

The Sun Goddess was represented by many symbols. One was the sun wheel—the Vedic swastika with its four "legs" that depicted the sun walking across the sky each day and blessing the Earth with her benevolent rays. Many examples on ancient pottery also represented the sun's rays as wavy or zig-zag lines flowing down from the eyes, mouth, and breasts of the Mother Goddess. Some rune casters have interpreted Sowilo's zig-zag shape to be a lightning bolt flashing down from a storm cloud. But lightning bolts and sun rays are two entirely different natural phenomena, and when we remember that the runes were originally made using only straight lines, we can also interpret Sowilo as an ideograph for an undulating ray of sunshine beaming down to kiss the earth. Sowilo represents success and confidence, to be sure, but it also signifies the light of truth reaching down to illuminate the dark corners of our lives, whether we welcome it or not. Sowilo asks, "Can you face the Truth?"

How does Sowilo help answer the question?

How could the glorious sun signify a challenge in your life? Isn't Sowilo all about acclaim and success, of you blazing forth brilliantly and being recognized for your abilities and accomplishments—your shining Self? The answer to both questions is "yes, but. . . ."

Are you being completely honest with yourself? Is there something you are not telling yourself or others? What does honesty have to do with the question? How might full disclosure impact the answer? And, on a deeper level, are self-criticism or self-doubt interfering with your ability to achieve your fullest potential in regards to the question being asked? A "dark" Sowilo might be suggesting that your self-deception is even deeper than you thought, or that it's time to come out of hiding. On the other hand, are others being honest with you?

But Sowilo has a great gift to offer those who endeavor to "know" themselves. For those who are strong and determined enough to explore their deepest wounds and confront their innermost demons, Sowilo can bestow the blessings of self-awareness. This can lead to the greatest accomplishment of all: self-compassion. If we can be compassionate with ourselves, then we can be compassionate with others. And, in the end, this is perhaps the most brilliant success of all.

The Crone Arc
Relationships

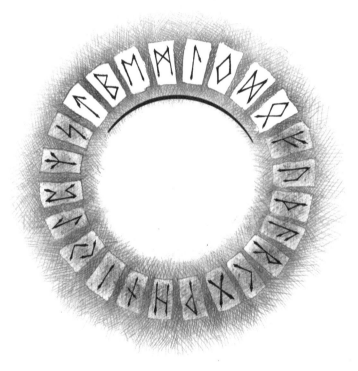

This final arc is that of the Crone; it contains the knowledge and blessings of a life of experience and seeks to connect us to and help us nurture our family, friends, and communities. Through the gifts of the Relationship Arc—guidance, support, partnership, unity, wisdom, fertility, opportunity, and totality—we are able to build strong relationships, create cohesive communities, and act with responsibility and integrity.

17. TEIWAZ, THE NORTH STAR: *GUIDANCE*

Like the compass needle it resembles, Teiwaz (*TIE-wahz*) signifies meaningful guidance, pointing us in the direction we want to go so we can fulfill our needs and commitments. In northern latitudes, our ancestors trusted the North Star to guide them across the land and over the seas to their destinations. As the old rune poem tells us:

> *Teiwaz is the guiding star.*
> *Well it keeps its faith with us on earth,*
> *Even over the mists of night, never failing.*

The North Star has long been a metaphor for trustworthy guidance. Like a good leader, it can be relied upon to guide us to our desired outcomes.

Guidance is advice that helps us reach a goal or solve a problem. We may ask someone for guidance because we believe they have knowledge or experience that is relevant to the situation, or because we feel we can trust them. And people may seek guidance from us for the same reasons.

Guidance is more than just giving advice, however. Guidance can also take the form of leadership, of shepherding a group toward a goal. Good leadership ensues when the people decide where they want to go and select the leaders they believe can help them get there. Thus good leadership has to be a cooperative endeavor. Furthermore, good leaders are not dictators who force their own will upon the people. Rather, good leaders continuously seek feedback from the group they are leading to make sure the people agree they are being guided in the direction they want to go.

The name Teiwaz comes from the Indo-European word *teiwa*, meaning "luminous being" or star. Teiwa originally referred to the Queen of Heaven, the Mother Goddess who looked after all beings on Earth and provided them with wise counsel. This belief in mystical astral guidance eventually led to the development of astrology, where the stars help us understand our past, present, and future.

As cultures evolved, the Queen of Heaven was dethroned and replaced by sky gods, and the figure called Teiwa, with her wise celestial guidance, was supplanted by bellicose characters like the Germanic war god Tiwaz and the Scandinavian war god Tyr. When Tyr first appeared in Norse mythology, he was an insignificant figure, and his only story tells of how he sacrificed his right hand in the Aesir gods' struggle to chain the mythic wolf Fenrir. As warrior culture grew, however, Tyr's sacrifice came to signify the attainment of justice. Consequently, the shape of the rune Teiwaz was reinterpreted as Tyr's spear of victory. But the shape of Teiwaz originally represented an arm pointing toward the stars or, later, a compass needle, suggesting where to look for guidance.

How does Teiwaz help answer the question?

There is rarely a situation in our complex world where we could not benefit from a little guidance. In the most positive sense, Teiwaz is telling you that the guidance you have received thus far has been good and has led you to your destination, or that you are going in the right direction to find the answer.

But Teiwaz may be suggesting that your question needs some North Star help. Who might this North Star be, and what kind of guidance could they provide? If it has landed "dark," it may be saying

84 ～ *Reading the Runes*

you feel lost and can't find the guidance you need, or that guidance is not available at this time. Are you seeking the right kind of guidance to answer your question? And can you accept it when it is offered?

Since Teiwaz refers to relationships, the rune might be pointing to a group's need for guidance. If so, perhaps you are the one being called upon to take up this responsibility. Are you prepared to assume a leadership role, and is Teiwaz *your* arm pointing the way?

18. BERKANA, THE SHE-BEAR: *SUPPORT*

Berkana (*bair-KAH-na*) is about nurturing something so it can develop to its fullest potential. The rune takes its name and meaning from the she-bear, who was an important totem animal to our ancestors, as evidenced by archaeological findings dating from as far back as 50,000 BCE. The she-bear was venerated as the creator and guardian of new life. Our ancestors observed that bear mothers were fearless and ferocious in defending their cubs. They were also tender mothers who lovingly and attentively cared for their young until they could fend for themselves. Figurines of "Bear Madonnas" unearthed at ancient ceremonial sites depict she-bears holding their cubs in their arms or carrying them in pouches on their backs.

Although usually thought to represent the letter B, the shape of Berkana perfectly illustrates this concept of support, for it is an ideograph of two breasts, the breasts of Mother Earth, symbolizing the source of nourishing sustenance. Breastfeeding is an apt metaphor for support. The "milk" of support flows out of one's interest in helping those beings, projects, or causes that need the involvement of others to ensure their success.

The name Berkana can be traced back to the Sanskrit words *bharati* and *khana*, which together suggest the act of carrying. In the Germanic language family, we find the Old High German word *beran* and the Old Norse word *bera*, both meaning to hold up or to bear, as in "to bear a burden." The word *bear* also came to refer to the large,

86 ~ *Reading the Runes*

powerful mammal of the Ursidae family, also called "the Brown One." What better animal to symbolize the idea of support than the she-bear herself, the devoted mother who nurtures her young?

Many goddesses had she-bear avatars. Perhaps the most well-known is the goddess Artemis. Called the "Lady of the Beasts," Artemis embodied the fecundity and regenerative powers of the Earth Mother, and she was the guardian of nature and wild animals. Artemis was represented most often by the bear, and her name was shared by other bear goddesses like Artio, the Mother of the Bear Clan of the Celts. Other European goddesses, such as Atargatis, Arco, and Arduinna, also had bear manifestations of ferocity in support of the young and vulnerable.

Artemis was also a moon goddess; the moon's waxing and waning cycle came to symbolize a woman's menstrual cycle and echo the energies of the female psyche and the limitless range of feminine possibility. Not surprisingly, Berkana is the one rune that rune casters agree represents feminine energy. We all possess feminine energy, regardless of our gender. As discussed earlier, one way to understand feminine energy is to see it as process energy—it flows through and supports everything we do each day, grounding us in the present and providing the basic foundation of our lives. Feminine energy is also what enables us to feel related to one another, to be receptive to the energies around us, and responsive to the needs that are being expressed by those of our community.

Another manifestation of feminine energy is parenting. Parenting—by both mothers and fathers—is not just about raising children. Parenting calls for nurturing others who need support and contributing to their development and well-being. Whenever we give support to our friends, family, or community, we are expressing Berkana energy.

How does Berkana help answer the question?

Berkana may be signaling that you are about to receive the support you need regarding the question you are asking. What kind of support might that be, and where would it be coming from? On the other hand, Berkana might be directing you to fulfill some form of "parenting" responsibility for someone else. Who is this person, and what kind of support might they need? If Berkana has landed "dark," it could mean that you can't see or accept the support that is there, and you feel that you are struggling alone.

Alternatively, Berkana could be alerting you to the birth of some new relationship or enterprise that is coming into your life, one that will need your support. Since Berkana refers to relationships, it might also be saying that your community needs support. Is there some project in need of money, resources, or labor?

Berkana, as the Rune of Feminine Energy, may be asking you to pay attention to how feminine energy impacts the question. Berkana might be telling you to seek the support of women, because their unique experience with the issue will help you answer the question in a deeper, more significant way.

19. EHWAZ, THE HORSE: *PARTNERSHIP*

Ehwaz (*AY-waz*) signifies the horse and its age-old partnership with humans. Domesticated some five thousand years ago, the horse was a partner to many of civilization's accomplishments. Indeed, the horse was so essential to society's success and its beauty and power so captured people's imaginations that, in time, it entered the realm of the gods as a divine being. Horse goddesses and other horse beings were found throughout Indo-European cultures, symbolizing a partnership between the Manifest and the Invisible Realms. For example, Horsel, the Teutonic moon goddess, passed through the night sky on her white moonlike mare, her waning and waxing phases representing the moon's essential partnership between dark and light that marked the passage of time.

Two mystical horses in Norse mythology were Hrimfaxi, "Sooty Mane," who pulled the night across the sky, and Shinfaxi, "Shiny Mane," who pulled the day, embodying the partnership of night and day. There was also Odin's horse, Sleipnir, the "Slipping One," who had eight legs, which many mythologists have thought signified great speed and agility and the power to carry Odin to other realms. But Sleipnir's eight legs originally depicted a partnership between two separate horses—the mare and the stallion—symbolizing the equal but opposite energies which had to be combined in order for life to proceed.

The name Ehwaz is derived from the German word *Ehe* (*AY-ah*), meaning a union or partnership. *Ehe* is the beginning syllable of the name of another divine equine, the pan-European horse goddess Epona (*ay-PO-na*), with *pona* meaning a small horse. Epona, a fertility and sovereignty goddess, was often depicted astride her white mare, holding a basket of fruits and grains that symbolized her fecundity. Epona's sovereignty signified her power over life and death, but this was shared power—power *with* humans rather than power *over* them. In this way, Epona embodied the profound partnership between the Mother Goddess and her people, with which they fulfilled their shared responsibilities of keeping society strong and cohesive.

A partnership is a conscious agreement between equals. It brings people together to accomplish a shared goal by combining their individual knowledge and strengths so they can work together as a team. The shape of the rune Ehwaz suggests a partnership. It is an ideograph of two individuals, standing side by side and holding hands, symbolizing their intentional union. Partnerships can form between individuals, or among groups of people. These relationships may be brief, to accomplish short-term goals, or ongoing, to achieve broad or generational aspirations. A partnership implies that mutual goals, mutual respect, and mutual reliance exist among the partners, and that their efforts are undertaken in service to their shared commitments.

How does Ehwaz help answer the question?

When Ehwaz appears in a casting, it is saying that the skills and energies of many people working together have something to do with answering the question. Ehwaz may be suggesting that team members are available who can rely on one another's strengths and shared commitments to successfully tackle the issue.

Who might these partners be? Who would want the enterprise to succeed? What are the various talents and strengths they could bring to the partnership? How will they benefit from working together rather than separately to achieve this goal? Are all the team members equally valued and respected? But if Ehwaz has landed "dark," it could mean that no partners are available.

Alternatively, you may feel that the idea of partnership or teamwork is unnecessary in regards to your question. If so, Ehwaz is telling you not to go it alone. You need to start looking around for allies to help you. That way, the burden will be shared, the rewards will be multiplied, and the whole community will be strengthened.

20. MANNAZ, THE HUMAN FAMILY: *UNITY*

When I was young, I traveled alone,
And wandered off the marked way.
Rich I thought myself when another person I found,
For humans are people's comfort.

These lines from the *Hávamál* (stanza 47) express the essential meaning of Mannaz (*MAHN-az*), the idea that the human community is precious to us. When we set aside differences like race, class, age, gender, nationality, culture, and language, we humans are all one species. The ways in which we communicate, ambulate, and procreate are only a few of the things that distinguish humans from the rest of creation and make us kin to each other. The human race is, after all, just one big family.

The name Mannaz comes from the German word *man*, meaning a person. Originally, man referred to the goddess Mann (*MAHN*), the Mother of All, and people called themselves Mankind—Kindred of Mann. This meant they were related to each other because they were all members of the Family of Mann. The shape of Mannaz confirms this concept; it is an ideograph of two people facing each other and acknowledging their kinship as fellow human beings. Mannaz also resembles two Wunjo runes, signifying "double joy," for joy is multiplied when people embrace each other as kin.

However, over many thousands of years we humans seem to have forgotten our inherent kinship with one another and have allowed

92   ~   *Reading the Runes*

all sorts of divisions to interfere with our natural relatedness. Where once we believed that we all shared in the divine lineage of the Mother Goddess, now we separate ourselves with racism, nationalism, politics, and religion. Even more troubling is that we have embraced the concept of "rugged individualism," where each of us is separate, like an island, and needs no one else to make us whole and complete. This perspective can ultimately lead to self-centeredness and self-absorption, and can bring with it arrogance, loneliness, and depression, as well as alienation and mistrust of other people.

Mannaz suggests that we reflect on our interconnectedness with the human race. When we look beyond our differences, what do we have in common? How can we focus on our similarities and our shared interests and needs? As human kindred, our own well-being is linked to the well-being of all the rest of humanity. The motto of Mannaz is, "we belong with you, and you belong with us," for as the *Hávamál* tells us "humans are people's comfort." In this regard, we might call Mannaz the Rune of Peace, for peace can bring us together as kin, and help us be members of the Family of Mankind.

How does Mannaz help answer the question?

Mannaz is sometimes also called the Rune of Belonging, that sense of being in the place where you want to be and among the people who claim you as their own. Belonging can bring great joy, comfort, safety and a sense of identity. What role does belonging play in answering your question?

Mannaz is also about kinship and relationships. How important is your family to you? Is the question referring to your birth family, or some "tribe" you feel you belong to? Mannaz might be saying that you already belong to a group, even if you don't realize it, and you need to shift your perspective and develop a more meaningful relationship with it. But if Mannaz has landed "dark," it could be saying that you feel you don't belong anywhere, or that the group you are with is not a good fit for you.

As the Rune of Peace, Mannaz could be suggesting that you should seek reunification and reconnect with whatever "family" you have drifted away from. It may also be pointing to the need to bring peace to an adversarial relationship. Will unity and peace help answer the question? If so, how might the other runes help attain these goals? Mannaz might also be telling you it is time to become active in issues of world peace and unity, since the rune resides in the Relationship Arc.

With kinship may come obligations, for the "family" is strengthened by the contributions of its members. Mannaz may be asking what your family needs from you.

21. LAGUZ, THE LAKE: *WISDOM*

Laguz (*LAH-gooz*) is the lake. A lake is defined as a large body of water surrounded by land. The surface of a lake changes constantly. It may be roughened by rain or wind, or smooth and glassy like a mirror, reflecting back all who gaze into it. But beneath its changeable surface, the lake is deep, dark, and mysterious because it holds within its shores the element of water. Since ancient times, water has been thought of as the conduit for wisdom—the wisdom of the Mother Goddess—and like water, wisdom's natural inclination is to flow. Wisdom takes the form of insight into the meaning of our existence, gained from lifetimes of reflecting on life and death. Wisdom is also discernment, the power to judge properly what is true and what is not.

The deep waters of lakes were thought to be the realm of the dead and the supernatural female beings who received the dead and prepared them for rebirth. The Germanic Mistress of the Wild was one such being who lived at the bottom of a deep lake that held the wisdom of the dead within its shores. The Anglo-Saxon tale of Beowulf told of the monster Grendel's mother, called *Grund Hyrde* or Ruler of the Depths, who lived in a mysterious lake and guarded the wisdom of the dead. And there was the fabled Lady of the Lake, who ruled the Celtic Land of the Dead that lay beneath the waters of her deep, dark lake.

The name *Laguz* comes from the German word *Lache* (*LAKH-ah*), meaning lake, and is related to another mystical lake-dweller, the goddess Laga. Laga was a divine being of such antiquity that no stories remain of her, and all we know about Laga is that her wisdom was so profound that Odin had to "wed" her so he could acquire her wisdom for himself.

The shape of Laguz has perplexed many rune casters, who generally interpret it as the crest of an ocean wave or the prow of a Viking ship. But ocean waves and Viking ships are images of the open seas, and they have little to do with lakes. Instead, Laguz is an ideograph of a mysterious, hooded figure, the Mistress of the Lake, shown rising up from her watery depths to speak her wisdom to those who wish to hear it.

The waters of the lake are also a symbol of intuitive knowing, a source of wisdom we all possess, though some of us may be more aware of it and more adept at accessing it than others. We may connect with our intuition as that "gut feeling" or "sixth sense" that helps us perceive things we don't experience with our five physical senses. Our intuition may take the form of clairvoyance (seeing things that are happening elsewhere) or clairaudience (hearing messages telepathically). We also tap into our intuitive wisdom when we seek information through divination.

But wisdom does not have to be mysterious or esoteric, because wisdom is also acquired naturally as we go through life, as we learn from and reflect on our lived experiences and our relationships with others. These reflections accumulate over time, for wisdom comes to those who pay attention and seek meaning from their lives. Wisdom is of value in itself, but its greatest worth comes when it is shared with others.

How does Laguz help answer the question?

The Wise Old Crone of Laguz has emerged from her watery depths. She is offering wisdom to help answer your question, wisdom that gives more than just an intelligent answer. Wisdom is that treasure from deep within, distilled from years, even generations, of experiencing and reflecting on life. Laguz is suggesting that you delve a little deeper into your question because then you will find an answer that is wise as well as practical.

Wisdom is always useful in our lives, though not always welcome, for it may be giving you a perspective you would rather not acknowledge. Laguz calls upon you to step back and see the bigger picture in order to figure out what is going on, for the wisdom represented by Laguz is best understood in the context of the broader situations, responsibilities, and relationships of our lives. But if Laguz is "dark," it could be saying that the answer you think is wise is merely sophomoric.

Wisdom is meant to be shared, otherwise it is just a dusty book on a shelf. Do you need to seek the wisdom of an elder in your community? What wisdom does the community need from you? Take a few moments to ponder, for wisdom may need some time to rise to the surface of its deep, dark lake.

Finally, since Laguz represents the element of water, it also refers to the emotions. Is there an emotional component to your question? Will examining the feelings that surround the question help you find the answer?

22. INGUZ, THE PORTAL: *FERTILITY*

Inguz (*ING-ooz*) signifies fertility, which is frequently defined as the ability to produce offspring. But fertility is more than just about making babies. It is the capacity for creating anything. There are fertile imaginations that produce literature, art, music, and philosophy, and there are fertile minds that invent tools, machines, and scientific theories.

But where does the urge to produce these things come from? It is often thought that fertility arises from the inspiration of one brilliant individual. However this explanation is very shortsighted. The urge to create arises from the aspirations of many people. It comes out of the Zeitgeist or "Spirit of the Age" that is calling for new ways of thinking and doing in the world. As the saying goes, "it takes two to tango," and unless a fertile mind is being stimulated by another fertile mind, fertility is just an abstract potential awaiting actualization.

Inguz represents the intersection of the fertility of many individuals. While one person may ultimately be credited with "inventing" something, that creation arose from a fomentation of the ideas, needs, trials and errors, and the hard work of many others who were driven by a similar vision. In the end, this vision is birthed through a group Portal, even if only one person gets the credit in the end.

The name of Inguz comes from the Teutonic fertility goddess Ingun, who was honored as the progenitor of the Ingvaeones, a Germanic tribe that inhabited Western Europe long before the

Roman invasion that occurred around two thousand years ago. When writing about the Germanic peoples, Tacitus, the Roman historian, mistakenly assumed that the powerful figure of Ingun was a male god. But Ingun was a Mother Goddess, as shown by the fact that many other fertility goddesses from that era shared her name. In Scandinavian cultures, she was known as Ingebjorg and Yngvi, and in Celtic regions she was called Yngova and Inghean Bhuide. The names of these goddesses were derived from the still older Indo-European concepts of yin, the principle of feminine energy, and yoni, the female sexual organ that symbolized the threshold between the womb and the world of the living—the Portal.

The Earth Mother's sacred yoni was represented by an image known as the Earth Diamond. The word diamond comes from the Latin *dia*, meaning goddess, and *mond*, meaning Earth—the Earth Goddess, out of whose Portal comes all of creation. The diamond's shape is made by taking a square, a classic earth symbol, and tipping it up on one of its corners so that it radiates vibrancy and creativity, the essential elements of fertility.

Some rune readers interpret the diamond shape of Inguz as the head of a penis or the scrotal sac of male genitalia. This interpretation limits fertility only to males because it alludes just to the male sexual acts of erection and ejaculation. On the other hand, we shouldn't confine our understanding of fertility only to the female elements of womb and egg. After all, it takes the uniting of both a female egg and a male sperm to create a fetus. But since we all emerge into the world through our mother's vulva, the Earth Diamond's sacred Portal pertains to everyone, regardless of what gender we claim as ours.

The fertility symbolized by Inguz is activated when the desires of many merge together. Inguz represents the coalescence of the creativity of many, so that together we can generate what we need and give birth to it through our collective Portal.

How does Inguz help answer the question?

Fertility may seem like a very personal topic, having to do with sexual intimacy or one's ability to conceive a child. Depending on the question being asked, Inguz might be suggesting just such a literal interpretation—the conception and birth of an infant.

But since fertility can relate to so many different things, you may need to take a broader perspective when you ask what Inguz has to do with the question. Is Inguz saying that creativity is needed in order to find an answer to the question? Could it be affirming that the creativity needed is indeed available, and just needs the collaboration of other people so that together you all can give birth to the solution through your communal Portal? Alternatively, if Inguz has shown up "dark," it might mean that the creative process has gone awry, that it's not the right time for the "birth" or the right elements are not available to construct the Portal.

What would building a community Portal look like? For example, could Inguz be referring to the need for a social, environmental, or political movement, the coming together of the concerns and energies of the many in order to "fertilize" a group solution? The other runes in the casting will show how such a Portal could be created.

23. DAGAZ, THE DAY: *OPPORTUNITY*

Dagaz (*DAHG-az*) comes from the German word *Dag*, meaning day. Dagaz represents the beautiful day, which awakens with the hopefulness of dawn, grows more magnificent with the glory of noon, and retires content with the fulfillment of dusk. But day is more than just the hours between sunrise and sunset. Day signifies our conscious awareness and our ability to act purposefully. Day is our natural element and our most comfortable domain. In the daytime we feel safe—while some might feel uneasy in the dark, who is afraid of the day? With day, all is possible because everything is clear, and it enables us to lead our most confident lives.

Dagaz signifies the opportunities that each day offers us, and when opportunity knocks, Dagaz urges us to open the door and go forth to meet it. After all, the motto of Dagaz is *Carpe Diem*—Seize the Day! But opportunities don't happen in a vacuum. They arise from things that are going on in the world around us, from the needs of friends, family, and community. It is our relationships with and responsibilities toward others that bring us these opportunities.

Dagaz was named for Dag, the Germanic goddess of day, whose brilliant ornament was the sun. Dag's magnificence was a projection of the Mother Goddess's love of the Earth and all its beings. In Germanic myth, Dag was the daughter of Nat, the Night, which is why each day is born at midnight, issuing from the mysterious darkness of her unfathomable womb. But as cultures came to assume that the child born at the Winter Solstice was male, Dag was eventually reinterpreted as the son of Nat.

The angular shape of Dagaz represents a butterfly with its wings outstretched in flight. The butterfly is a universal symbol for the soul, and signifies the soul's infinite possibilities. And since the straight lines of runes were sometimes meant to represent curved lines, the shape of Dagaz can also be seen as a lemniscate—the perpetually looping figure-eight or infinity symbol. The lemniscate suggests life's endless opportunities to reach goals and fulfill dreams. As eighteenth-century Scottish writer Thomas Carlyle wrote in his poem, "Today": "So here hath been dawning / Another blue Day: / Think wilt thou let it / Slip useless away." Dagaz urges you to go forth and pursue that butterfly, that symbol of opportunity.

How does Dagaz help answer the question?

Dagaz is a positive rune, bringing with it the symbolic brilliance and hope of a new day. It is signaling the emergence of an opportunity for you—something to celebrate. And if the question is asking about a specific opportunity, Dagaz is indicating a good outcome.

Seeing Dagaz from a broader perspective may also help explain what kind of opportunity Dagaz is offering. For example, literally interpreted, Dagaz could mean something is going to happen on this particular day, or that daytime has special meaning to the question, as opposed to nighttime.

If Dagaz is "dark," it might be warning that this is not a real opportunity, or it is a bad one for you, or maybe you aren't able to follow through on it, even when it is being directly offered. There could be any number of reasons for this reluctance. Perhaps you are just not prepared at this time. The other runes will help to identify and explain any roadblocks in your way.

24. OTHALA, THE HOMELAND: *TOTALITY*

Othala (*OH-tha-la*) is the richest and most complex of all the runes. It symbolizes the Earth-based spirituality principle that "everything is everything." Othala signifies the totality of our existence in all of its dimensions. It is a wholly positive rune.

The name Othala comes from the Old Norse word, *odhal* (*OH-thal*), meaning homeland. Homeland can be a divisive term that separates us from one another based on where our ancestors came from, or the place we now call home. But the homeland signified by Othala is infinitely larger than these narrow, human-made definitions, for Othala's homeland refers to Mother Earth herself—this vast body of soil and rock upon which we all live. Furthermore, our ancestors believed that the Earth is the Mother of All Beings, not just humans. And they observed that she does not favor one form of life over another, but makes a place for all beings according to their needs. She holds them close to her bosom with her gravitational pull, so that even the birds of the air must return to her embrace.

Although Othala's shape is angular, the top part of the symbol is meant to signify a circle, an ancient symbol for the Earth and for life's inclusiveness. Since ancient times, the circle has been known as the Sacred Enclosure. This is the universal ceremonial space whose circumference contains everything and whose center is everywhere. Within the Sacred Enclosure, all are equal because a circle has no higher or lower positions. While the Sacred Enclosure exists everywhere at all times, we consciously invoke it when we want to create a container to hold the energy we raise in ceremony.

The Sacred Enclosure is also the realm where we celebrate the Ceremony of Life—the joy of being alive in all of life's dimensions. Great wealth abounds in the Sacred Enclosure: the wealth of love, self-acceptance and compassion for others, of being aware of our existence on the Manifest Plane of physical being as well as the incorporeal Plane of Spirit. In the Sacred Enclosure, we experience the ecstasy of being connected to everything all at once.

The two lines that reach down from Othala's "circle" represent the roots of attachment that all beings have to Mother Earth. Othala asks us to be aware of the land that lies beneath our feet and stretches out in all directions. Othala urges us to develop our sensitivity to the Earth's telluric energy—to the ley lines that run along its surface, and to the atmospheric manifestations that flow above it.

Othala's downward pointing lines also link us to the ancestors, to all those who have gone before us and imbued the land with their lived experiences. Othala connects us to the vastness of the past and to the limitlessness of the future. It reminds us that we ourselves will be the ancestors of tomorrow; therefore we must be mindful of how we are walking upon Mother Earth and consider what legacies we ourselves will be handing down to future generations.

On an even deeper level, Othala signifies totality. What does totality mean in the context of our lives? It means that we exist simultaneously in the multiple dimensions of time, the material world, the metaphysical realm, and the Divine. Whatever fears and lack of awareness we have that separate us from the rest of the world dissolve in the presence of Othala, and we are awakened to our connection with all that is. We join the joyous Ceremony of Life, while residing at its peaceful center.

How does Othala help answer the question?

When Othala shows up in a rune casting, its presence might seem a little overwhelming because it symbolizes the entirety of existence. It is a wholly positive rune, however, and can bring with it happiness beyond words and the ecstatic awareness that you are connected to all that is.

While the appearance of Othala is signaling the successful outcome of the question being asked, you will need to look beyond the specific outcome you are seeking and visualize the ultimate unity this outcome can bring to your life and the world around you. How does this totality give you access to the joy of your True Self, that core of unity with all of life? Othala is asking you to be open to your inherent divinity, and thus to the Divine in all of its expressions. It could be signaling that you are about to experience a great epiphany.

On a mundane level, however, Othala could be suggesting the purchase of land, or have something to do with land that you are already associated with or your responsibilities to the land. Othala could also be pointing to your ancestors. How might the ancestors impact your question? Could Othala be suggesting that you have some responsibility to future generations?

What if Othala has landed "dark" or is covered by other runes? In the case of other runes, this might be warning you that some factor is getting in the way of a rune's meaning. But in the case of Othala, this obstructive element is most likely yourself. The most likely negative connotation of a "dark" or covered Othala is that, for some reason, you are not able to perceive your place in the totality of existence and therefore are unable to fully participate in it. It's there, but you just can't see it. Othala could be telling you to open your eyes, for when you are able to see your place in the Sacred Enclosure, you will be able to fully participate in the ecstatic Ceremony of Life.

CONCLUSION

I wrote this book at the request of my students because they told me they couldn't find the information I was teaching in other books about the runes. Indeed, unlike other rune books, this one is based on the meanings of the runes as symbols of Earth-based spirituality and the Earth Mother, a perspective rooted in ecofeminism and the sacredness of the Earth.

As this book endeavors to show, Earth-based spirituality has two basic tenets. First, Spirit dwells in the here and now, not off in some supernatural dimension. Second, Spirit dwells in all beings, both human and nonhuman, as well as in natural phenomena, like earth and water, wind and rain, and the moon, sun, and stars. And since Spirit dwells in everything, this means everything is related to everything else.

How does Earth-based spirituality help us interpret rune castings? Each rune that shows up in a casting links the question being asked to the vastness of "All My Relations," to reference a Native American expression. This awareness moves us beyond a mundane understanding of the rune casting and offers us access to Mother Earth, whose wisdom is present in each rune. And you, the rune reader, are the one who explains those deeper, Earth-based meanings and reminds us of our relatedness to All That Is.

I hope you have found this book helpful, not only by embellishing your skills for reading the runes, but also by offering you new ways for seeing the world and your place in it.

May all your readings be true.

BIBLIOGRAPHY

Ann, Martha, and Dorothy Myers Imel. *Goddesses in World Mythology: A Bibliographical Dictionary*. Oxford University Press, 1993.

Aswynn, Freya. *Northern Mysteries & Magick: Runes & Feminine Powers*. Llewellyn Publications, 1990.

Baring, Anne, and Jules Cashford. *Myth of the Goddess: Evolution of an Image*. Arkana Penguin Group, 1991.

Briffault, Robert. *The Mothers: The Matriarchal Theory of Social Origins*. Universal Library, 1963.

Chinn, Peggy L. *Peace and Power: Creative Leadership of Building Community*, 6th ed. Jones and Bartlett, 2008.

Circlot, J. E. *Dictionary of Symbols*. Philosophical Library, 1983.

Cooper, J. C. *Illustrated Encyclopedia of Traditional Symbols*. Thames and Hudson, 1978.

Cooper, J. C. *Symbolic & Mythological Animals*. Aquarian/Thorsons, 1992.

Davidson, H. R. Ellis. *Gods and Myths of Northern Europe*. Penguin Books, Ltd, 1964.

Davidson, H. R. Ellis. *Pagan Scandinavia: Ancient Peoples and Places*. Thames and Hudson, 1967.

Davidson, H. R. Ellis. *Myths and Symbols in Pagan Europe*. Syracuse University Press, 1988.

Davidson, H. R. Ellis. *The Lost Beliefs of Northern Europe*. Barnes & Noble, 1993.

Davidson, H. R. Ellis. *Roles of the Northern Goddess*. Routledge, 1998.

Dixon-Kennedy, Mike. *Celtic Myth & Legend*. Blandford, 1997.

108 ～ *Bibliography*

Downing, Christine. *The Goddess: Mythological Images of the Feminine.* Crossroad Publishing, 1988.

Eisler, Riane. *Chalice and the Blade: Our History, Our Future.* Perennial Library/ Harper & Row, 1987.

Eller, Cynthia. *The Myth of Matriarchal Prehistory.* Beacon Press, 2000.

Elliott, Ralph W. V. *Runes: An Introduction.* Manchester University Press, 1959.

Gilligan, Carol. *In a Different Voice: Psychological Theory and Women's Development.* Harvard University Press, 1982.

Gimbutas, Marija. *Civilization of the Goddess: The World of Old Europe.* Harper San Francisco, 1991.

Gimbutas, Marija. *Goddesses and Gods of Old Europe: Myths and Cult Images.* University of California Press, 1982.

Gimbutas, Marija. *The Language of the Goddess.* Harper San Francisco, 1989.

Goodison, Lucy, and Christine Morris, eds. *Ancient Goddesses: The Myths and the Evidence.* British Museum Press, 1998.

Green, Miranda. *Celtic Goddesses: Warriors, Virgins, and Mothers.* British Museum Press, 1995.

Grimm, Jacob. *Teutonic Mythology,* Volumes 1–4. Translated by James Steven Stallybrass. Dover, 1966.

Hageneder, Fred. *The Meaning of Trees: Botany, Healing, History, Lore.* Chronicle Books, 2005.

Hogan, Linda, Deena Metzger, and Brenda Peterson, eds. *Intimate Nature: The Bond Between Women and Animals.* Fawcett Columbine, 1998.

James, E. O. *Cult of the Mother-Goddess.* Barnes & Noble, 1994.

Johnson, Buffie. *Lady of the Beasts: Ancient Images of the Goddess and Her Sacred Animals.* Harper & Row, 1988.

Kinsley, David. *The Ten Mahavidyas: Tantric Visions of the Divine Feminine.* University of California Press, 1997.

Lesko, Barbara S. *The Great Goddesses of Egypt.* University of Oklahoma Press, 1999.

Lindow, John. *Norse Mythology: A Guide to the Gods, Heroes, Rituals, and Beliefs.* Oxford University Press, 2001.

MacKillop, James. *Dictionary of Celtic Mythology.* Oxford University Press, 1998.

Markale, Jean. *The Great Goddess: Reverence of the Divine Feminine from the Paleolithic to the Present.* Inner Traditions, 1999.

Bibliography 109

McCoy, Edain. *Celtic Myth & Magick*. Llewellyn Publications, 1995.

Meadows, Kenneth. *Rune Power*. Castle Books, 2002.

Monaghan, Patricia. *Book of Goddesses & Heroines*. Llewellyn Publications, 1993.

Monaghan, Patricia. *O Mother Sun! A New View of the Cosmic Feminine*. The Crossing Press, 1994.

Neumann, Erich. *The Great Mother: An Analysis of the Archetype*. Translated by Ralph Manheim. Princeton University Press, 1972.

Noddings, Nell. *Caring: A Feminine Approach to Ethics & Moral Education*. University of California Press, 1984.

Page, R. I. *Introduction to English Runes*. Methuen, 1973.

Page, R. I. *Norse Myths*. British Museum Press, 1990.

Patai, Raphael. *The Hebrew Goddess*. Wayne State University Press, 1978,

Paxson, Diana L. *Taking Up the Runes*. Weiser Books, 2005.

Pollack, Rachel. *Seventy-Eight Degrees of Wisdom: A Book of Tarot*. Thorsons, 1997.

Shlain, Leonard. *The Alphabet Versus the Goddess: The Conflict Between Word and Image*. Arkana Penguin Group, 1998.

Simek, Rudolf. *Dictionary of Northern Mythology*. Translated by Angela Hall. D. S. Brewer, 1993.

Sjoo, Monica, and Barbara Mor. *The Great Cosmic Mother: Rediscovering the Religion of the Earth*. Harper San Francisco, 1987.

Stone, Merlin. *When God Was a Woman*. Dorset Press, 1976.

Thorsson, Edred. *Runelore*. Weiser Books, 1987.

Turville-Petre, E. O. G. *Myth and Religion of the North*. Weidenfeld and Nicholson, 1964.

Walker, Barbara G. *Woman's Dictionary of Symbols & Sacred Objects*. Harper, 1988

Walker, Barbara G. *Woman's Encyclopedia of Myths and Secrets*. Harper, 1983.

Wolkstein, Diane, and Samuel Noah Kramer. *Inanna: Queen of Heaven and Earth*. Harper & Row Publishers, 1987.

INDEX

Aditi, 34

Aesir, 37

aett, links to deities, 5

aettir divisions of runes, 5, 28. *See also*
Crone arc; Maiden arc; Mother
arc

agency, 40–42

Alagabiae, 49

Algiz, 74–76
dark Algiz, 75–76
derivation of term, 75
how does it help answer the
question? 75–76

Allgegenwart, 75

allgewaltig, 75

"All My Relations," 105

an, defined, 40

Ansuz, 24, 40–42
dark Ansuz, 42
derivation of term, 40
how does it help answer the
question?, 41–42

Arco, 86

Arduinna, 86

Arianrhod, 43

Artemis, 86

Artio, 86

Aryan symbols, runes as, 2

Asgard, 56

Atargatis, 86

Audumla, 34–35

aurochs, 34–35

Axis Mundi, 14

Baba Yaga, 72

bear, derivation of term, 85–86

Bear Madonnas, 85

Beiwe, 32

Belonging, Rune of, 91–93

Beowulf, 94

beran, 85

Berchta, 72

Berkana, 23, 85–87
dark Berkana, 87
how does it help answer the
question?, 86–87

112　～　*Index*

bharati, 85
Bifrost, 56
Bird Mother, 74–75
Birthright arc, 6, 29–39
bow drill, the, 60
Braugi, 10
breastfeeding, 85
"bright" runes, *21*
　defined, 21
Bugady Musan, 32
butterfly, 101

Carlyle, Thomas, 101
Carpe Diem, 100
casting, defined, 17
casting the runes, 17–26
　as ceremony, 17–18
　clumped together runes, 22–23,
　　22
　creating the question, 19
　defined, 17
　example, 18, *18*, 23–25
　noticing the arc of each rune, 23
　overlapping runes, 22–23
　process of casting, 20–25
　selecting the tools, 19–20
　when one lands on edge, 22
　why we cast, 25–26
cauldron, and Perthro, 71–73
cave paintings, 35
Ceremony of Life, 103
Cerridwen, 72
Challenge arc, 6, 55–79
Chokmah, 41
Communication, Rune of, 40–42

Crone arc, 23, 81–104
　defined, 6
cycle, defined, 65

Dag, 60, 100
Dagaz, 100–101
　dark Dagaz, 101
　derivation of term, 100
　how does it help answer the
　　question?, 101
dark runes, 21–22, *21*
　defined, 21
　interpreting, 22
Day, 100–101
death, and Eihwaz, 68–70
Death Rune, 68–70
Defense, Rune of, 74–76
desire, and wishing, 52–54
diaspora, 3
Disa, 32
Disir, 63
disruption, Hagelaz and, 56–58
divination, defined, 17
Divine Creator, as Mother, 7–8

Earth
　as giver, 49
　sacredness of the, 105
　as source of wisdom, 20
Earth-based spirituality, 3, 8, 102,
　105
Earth Diamond, 98
Earth Mother, 7, 14, 37, 86, 98, 105.
　See also Mother Goddess
ecofeminist perspective on runes, 3

Index ～ 113

Ehwaz, 88–90
  dark Ehwaz, 90
  derivation of term, 88–89
  how does it help answer the
    question?, 89–90
Eihwaz, 25, 68–70
  derivation of term, 68
  how does it help answer the
    question?, 69–70
Elder Futhark, 4–5
Elhaz, 75
Eo-Anu, 69
Eoh, 69
epiphany, 48
Epona, 89
eye, the, 46–48
Eye Goddess, 46–47
eye surgery casting, 23–25, 24

Fairy Flag, 53
Fairy Godmother, 53
family, 91–93
Fehu, 30–33, 31
  dark Fehu, 33
  derivation of term, 30
  how does it help answer the
    question?, 32–33
feminine energy, 7–8
  three "Rs" of, 7
Feminine Energy Rune (Berkana),
    85–87
Fenrir, 83
fertility, 97–99
Fertility Rune, 97–99
fight or flight tendency, 8

freezing, 62–63
Futhark
  derivation of term, 4
  described, 4–5

Gebjon, 49
Gebo, 49–51
  derivation of term, 49
  how does it help answer the
    question?, 50–51
Gefn, 49
giants, the, 37–39
  described, 37–39
giver (Gebo), 49–51
goal energy, 8
Goddess. See Mother Goddess
Goddess Hel, 14
God of Battle, Odin as, 9
God of Magic, Odin as, 9
gratitude, 49–51
Great Cauldron, 71
Great Unknown, 71
Grund Hyrde, 94
guidance, 82–84
  defined, 82
Guidance Rune, 82–84
Gunnlod, 10
gynocratic societies, 15

Hagelaz, 23, 56–58
  dark Hagelaz, 58
  defined, 56
  derivation of term, 56
  how does it help answer the
    question?, 57–58

114 ～ *Index*

Hageneder, Fred, 68
hail (Hagelaz), 56–58
Harvest, Rune of, 66
Hathor, 34
Hávamál, 9, 11, 91
health, 34–36
Health, Rune of, 34–36
Heimdallr, 56
Hera, 34
Hesiod, 13
"History of the Goddess" course, 15
"Holy Grail," 48
homeland, 102–4
honesty, 78–79
horse, 88–90
Horsel, 88
"How shall I get there?", 43–44
Hrimfaxi, 88
human beings, origins of, 3
human family, 91–93
Hvergelmir, 71

"I Am," 77
ice, 62–64
Ierne, 69
immobility, 62–64
Indo-European languages, 3
Ingebjorg, 98
Inghean Ghuide, 98
Ingun, 97–98
Inguz, 97–99
    dark Inguz, 99
    how does it help answer the
        question?, 99
instincts, in understanding runes, 26
intuition, 95

Isa, 62–64
    defined, 62
    derivation of term, 62
    how does it help answer the
        question?, 63–64
Isis, 34
Iwa, 68

Jara, 65
Jera, 23–24, 65–67
    derivation of term, 65
    how does it help answer the
        question?, 66–67
Jerah, 65
journeys, 45

Kenaz, 23, 46–48
    dark Kenaz, 48
    derivation of term, 46
    how does it help answer the
        question?, 47–48
khana, 85
knowing, Kenaz and, 46–48
Knowing, Rune of, 46–48
"Know Thyself," 77
kundalini, 47

Lady of the Lake, 94
Laga, 94–95
Laguz, 24, 94–96
    dark Laguz, 96
    derivation of term, 94–95
    how does it help answer the
        question?, 95–96
lake (Laguz), 94
leadership, 82–84

Index ～ 115

Life, Rune of, 32
luck, 60–61
Luck, Rune of, 61

Maat, 47
Magic, Rune of, 52–54
Maiden arc, 23, 29–39
  defined, 5–6
male energy, 8
Mankind, 91
Mannaz, 91–93
  dark Mannaz, 92
  derivation of term, 91
  how does it help answer the
    question?, 92–93
Marriage Rune, 51
mattr ok megin, 44
Mead of Inspiration, 10–11
Meldorf Brooch, 2
Midgard, 56
Midgard Serpent, 63
might makes right ethic, 15
Mistress of the Lake, 95
Mistress of the Wild, 94
Mjotvidr, *12*, 13–14, 68–69
Mother arc, 23, 55–79
  defined, 6
Mother Earth, 102
Mother Goddess, 83
  described, 7–8
  Mouthpiece of the, 40–42
  reclaiming runes for the, 1–26, 28
  societies of the, 15–16
  and Tantrism, 47
  and Teiwa, 83
  as war goddess, 74

Mother Holle, 72
Mother Serpent, 63
Mother Tree, 13–14
Mouthpiece of the Goddess, 40–42
Mystery, Rune of, 71–73

Nat, 60
Naudhiz, 59–61
  dark Naudhiz, 60–61
  derivation of term, 59
  how does it help answer the
    question?, 60–61
need, and want, 59
Need-Fire Rune, 59
night, as Mother of the Gods, 13
nine, as sacred number, 13
Noddings, Nell, 7
North Star, 82–84

Odin, 8
  under Christianity, 11
  described, 9–11
  Mead of Inspiration stolen by,
    10–11
  as relative newcomer, 10
  winning the runes, 11–13
Odin-centric mythology, and runes, 8
Odin's prize, 9
ogham, 69
Opportunity Rune, 100–101
orlog, 44
Oskmeyjar, 53
Othala, 25, 102–4
  dark Othala, 104
  how does it help answer the
    question?, 104

116 ～ *Index*

parenting, 86
partnership, 88–90
Partnership Rune, 88–90
patriarchal regimes, 15–16
Peace, Rune of, 92–93
People of the Yew, 69
Perchta, 71
Perthro, 71–73
  derivation of term, 71
  how does it help answer the
    question?, 72–73
Portal, 97–99
Primal Cow, described, 34–35
Protection, Rune of, 38
purpose, 43–45

question
  creating the, 19
  specific vs. vague, 19

Raidho, 25, 43–45
  dark Raidho, 44–45
  derivation of term, 43
  how does it help answer the
    question?, 44–45
Rainbow Bridge, 56
reading the runes, 27–104
receptiveness, defined, 7
reclaiming runes for the Goddess,
  1–26
  as purpose of the book, 3
reindeer, 30–32
  revered as gods, 30–32
  veneration of the doe, 32
Reindeer Era, 30
Reindeer Mother (Fehu), 30–33, *31*

relatedness, defined, 7
Relationship arc, 6, 81–104
responsiveness, defined, 7
rugged individualism, 92
rune cloth, 19–20
runes, the. *See also* casting the runes
  aettir divisions of, 5
  as Aryan symbols, 2
  deeper meanings of, 6–7
  defined, 4
  as "embryonic writing"?, 4
  oldest known, 2
  origin of, 2–7
  reading, 27–104
  reclaiming for the Goddess,
    1–26
  representing esoteric concepts,
    4
  theft of, 13–16
  today, 4–6
  understanding, 25–26
  to whom did they originally belong?,
    13–14
Ruskin, John, 32

Sacred Enclosure, 102-3
Sar-akka, 32
Sarasvati, 41
Saule, 78
savoir faire, in the Crone arc, 6
Schwan, 75
"seeing is believing," 46
self-compassion, 79
self-doubt, 77–79
sexuality, and Kenaz, 47
she-bear (Berkana), 85–87

Shinfaxi, 88
Sleipnir, 88
Sol, 78
Sophia, 41
Sowilo, 77–79
    dark Sowilo, 79
    derivation of term, 78
    how does it help answer the
        question?, 78–79
spamadr, 41
Spirit
    dwells in all beings, 105
    as here and now, 105
    the voice of, 42
Sturleson, Snorri, 9
Sulis, 47, 78
Sun Mother, 78
Sunna, 78
Sun Rune, 77–79
Support Rune, 85–87
Suttungr, 10
swan, and Algiz, 74–76
Swan Maidens, 75

Tantric practice, 47
Teiwaz, 25, 82–84
    dark Teiwaz, 83–84
    derivation of term, 83
    how does it help answer the
        question?, 83–84
tend and befriend impulse, 7–8
theft of the runes, 13–16
Thurisaz, 37–39
    dark Thurisaz, 38–39
    derivation of term, 37
    helps us inhabit the world, 38

how does it help answer the
    question?, 38–39
time, 65–67
Time Management, Rune of,
    66
Tiwaz, 83
tool selection, 19–20
totality, 102–4
Totality Rune, 102–4
Tree of Life, 69. *See also* Mjotvidr
Truth, Rune of, 77–79
Tyr, 83

unity, 91–93
Uruz, 34–36
    dark Uruz, 35–36
    derivation of term, 34
    how does it help answer the
        question?, 35–36

Vac, 40–41
vagina, and Kenaz, 47
voice, 40–42

wands, 53
want, and need, 59
war goddess, 74
water, and wisdom, 94, 96
wealth, defined, 30
Wealth, Rune of, 30–33
wealth rune, 30–33
wheel, 43–45
    as symbol, 43
"Where do I want to go?", 43–44
"Who am I?", 77
Wild Hunt, 71–72

Index

wisdom, 94–96
  and water, 94, 96
Wisdom Rune, 94–96
wish, the, 52–54
  method of making, 52
"wish me luck," 60
Wish Rune, 52–54
World Serpent, 63
Wunjo, 52–54
  derivation of term, 52
  how does it help answer the
    question?, 53–54

"X" shape, 49–50

year, the, 65–67
yew trees, 68–70
  symbolism of, 68
Yggdrasil, 13–14
Ymir, 34
Yngova, 98
Yngvi, 98

Zeitgeist, defined, 97